The 15-Ounce Pound

Big Pharma's Plan to Patent Pot

Joseph R. Pietri

Published by:

Trine Day LLC
PO Box 577
Walterville, OR 97489
1-800-556-2012
www.TrineDay.com
publisher@TrineDay.net

Library of Congress Control Number: 2014932059

Pietri, Joseph

The 15 Ounce Pound—1st ed.
p. cm.
Includes references and index.
Epud (ISBN-13) 978-1-937584-15-3
Mobi (ISBN-13) 978-1-937584-16-0
Print (ISBN-13) 978-1-937584-14-6
1. Marijuana industry -- United States. 2. Marijuana industry -- Netherlands 3. Pharmaceutical industry -- United States. 4. Marijuana Smoking
-- legislation & jurisprudence -- United States. I. Pietri, Joseph . II. Title

First Edition

10 9 8 7 6 5 4 3 2 1

Printed in the USA
Distribution to the Trade by:
Independent Publishers Group (IPG)
814 North Franklin Street
Chicago, Illinois 60610
312.337.0747
www.ipgbook.com

Enjoying the bliss.

Om Shiva Shankara Hari Hari Ganja!
Boom Somnath!

There's somethin' happenin' here
What it is ain't exactly clear
There's a man with a gun over there
A tellin' me, I got to beware
I think it's time we stop, children, what's that sound?
Everybody look what's going down

Origin of the term POT

Moroccan gentlemen have traditionally kept their smoking herbs in a small ceramic containers. The wise old men of the village are commonly blessed with the saying, "May his pipe and pot always be within reach."

Special thanks to Lord Shiva who guides me, and to Kris my publisher who toned down my anger all this information gave me. To Ray Cogo, John Chick RIP, Dan Boughen, Hollyweed Dragon, Bret Brogue and Curry Ojeda for inspiration, to Joe Adams for running the farm, to Wernard Bruining for photos, and special thanks to Peter McGuire, and Reinhard Delp and family

Table of Contents

Foreword

During the past year a new realism has entered the debate over marijuana legalization. Not only did CNN's trusted Dr. Shanjay Gupta do a complete 180 and denounce his previous statements about pot, President and one time "Choom Gang" member Barack Obama recently stated in an interview that he considered pot no more dangerous than cigarettes and alcohol. Attorney General Eric Holder's recent decision to allow banks to launder marijuana money, coupled with the legalization of recreational pot in Colorado provide further evidence that the American government's unconditional surrender in the war on marijuana is near. Like the Nixon administration during the waning days of the Vietnam War, the Obama administration is looking for a clean exit from the war on pot, but there is none. The U.S. government has lost the War on Drugs and now must face its toxic progeny: a prison industrial complex, a two-tiered judicial system and an out of control pharmaceutical industry whose opiates kill more people each year than all illegal drugs combined. If this is the war its proponents once bragged it was, it will be counted as one of the great pyrrhic victories in military history.

Without question, the most costly and pointless battle in this war was fought against marijuana. Cannabis is probably the most useful plant on earth, but because one of its one thousand molecules is intoxicating, the entire species has been outlawed for almost a century. During the decades of pot prohibition, massive commercial hemp farms were replaced by tiny clandestine gardens whose tradecraft and strain genetics were closely held secrets. The illegal marijuana industry is one of the best examples of economist Adam Smith's "invisible hand" at work, and provides empirical proof that political laws will always be less powerful than the economic law of supply and demand. With the legalization of American marijuana imminent, big pharma and their hand-picked allies in the pot trade are attempting to establish a marijuana monopoly. The future looks sadly familiar.

Joseph Pietri's *The 15-Ounce Pound* is a timely and important book. The author's investigation of the ominous alliance of Horta-Pharm, GW Pharmaceuticals, and Bayer A.G. provides yet another example of a corporate consolidation that will attempt to destroy or swallow all competition. Should big pharma be allowed to patent a plant that has been used medicinally by non-industrial cultures for centuries? The story of cannabis industry pioneer Reinhard Delp is a sad and cautionary tale that should inspire the former black marketers, those who ran the greatest risks and paid the greatest price, to resist the corporate takeover of American marijuana.

One response to *The 15-Ounce Pound* will be predictable. Joseph Pietri will be called "DEA informant," "rat" and "snitch" as he has in the past for pointing out uncomfortable facts. However, these are just *ad hominem* attacks; his critics will strenuously avoid the substance of Pietri's argument because he is correct about the confused state of legal marijuana in the United States and throughout the world. Big pharma, DEA insiders, and Wall Street kleptocrats should not be allowed determine the future of legal marijuana.

– Dr. Peter Maguire
June 1, 2014

CHAPTER 1

When you go into the jungle, don't talk to the monkeys – go directly to Tarzan.

It was rainy and gray when I landed in Amsterdam from Oregon for the 19th *High Times* Cannabis Cup in November of 2006. After getting through the airport maze I hopped on a trolley into town. I had booked a room at the last minute; when I got there it was a fifth floor walk-up, no elevator and my room was on the top floor. I carried my books, luggage, and equipment, and fell out on the bed.

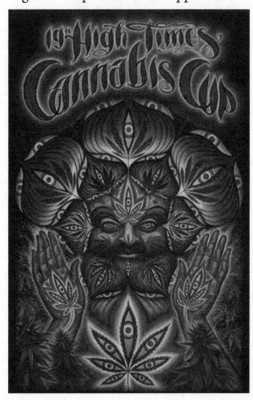

My new book *The King of Nepal: Ice-Wars Edition* was fresh off the presses, and I intended to introduce it at the Cup. I also had an XTR 1000, a new hash-making machine, which I planned to demonstrate at the Cup. My thoughts raced back to Viola, the inventor's wife who had warned me to be careful; none of them would even dare to go to Holland for fear of being killed.

The next day I lugged all my gear over to the venue, which was held on an industrial island just across from Amsterdam, so we had to cross over on a ferry. The venue was small, a hassle to get to, but we had rented a premier booth on the stage, a top spot. Kelly Kriston, founder of KDK Wholesale and I shared a booth. We set up our booth, and Arjan's Greenhouse donated cannabis for the XTR 1000 demonstration. I was all set up at the Holy Grail of weed, the Cannabis Cup.

Over the years, it has been whispered amongst the cannabis community that *High Times'* annual Cannabis Cup was rigged and an overall fraud. *Cannabis Culture*, a Canadian publication and competitor to *High Times*, extensively documented what they viewed to be corruption, favoritism and rigged outcomes at the Cannabis Cups they observed.

In the booth next to me was DNA Genetics. The company had entered their Martian Mean Green in the cup. They offered us a bag of the worst schwagg I had seen in quite a while.

The first day started with meeting and greeting. I was selling books, and folks were getting high on some hash that I had made. Everybody told me it was the best they had ever smoked in Amsterdam.

Steve Hager

Although cannabis was never truly legal in Amsterdam, it was tolerated by law enforcement as requested by city officials. Laws were never changed at the city or national level, so the legal consequences could be re-applied any time.

What blossomed in Amsterdam was quite remarkable. The coffee shops began selling marijuana over the counter. Word got out and the tourist dollars poured in. The idea of the Cannabis Cup came to *High Times* editor Steve Hager in 1987, or so the story goes. The first Cup was held in 1988.

In my *Ice Wars Edition*, I had added a "bombshell" chapter in which I detailed what I believed to be a fraud committed by a cabal of David Watson, Robert C. Clarke, Mila Jansen and others regarding an ice water hash-making method, which had been developed and then later officially patented in December of 2000, by Reinhard C. Delp. He had filed for his patent in February of

the
KinG Of
NepaL

ICE WARS EDITION

My book that I published and then distributed at the 2006 Cannabis Cup.

Joseph R. Pietri

1997, and it was a very significant and important breakthrough in hash-making processing. It involved washing the plant in ice water to separate the resin glands – the "medicine."

The cabal "stole" Delp's invention, and with the help of *High Times* and the rest of the cannabis community, wittingly or unwittingly, created a "myth," which has been presented as factually true.

The next day, I was just starting to sign books when I noticed in the corner of my eye, someone eyeing me. He was tall and built like

Lester Grinspoon. M.D.

David Watson

a pro football player, and then suddenly he darted towards me in an extremely threatening manner.

"You blew my cover," David Watson blared.

He was staring at me like a boxer at a contentious weigh-in.

Kriston from KDK Wholesale, who was even more buff than Watson stepped in.

"Everything OK?" Kriston asked

Watson looked at Kriston and backed off.

Within hours Watson put up wanted posters with my face on it all around the Cup, implying I was a narc.

Paranoia set in, but I stood my ground, never leaving my booth. I was told later that Watson had offered to buy my booth space at the Cup.

I pressed on with my book sales.

Hager remained eerily silent.

A lady named Zoe, approached and gave me a hard time about my *Ice Wars* book, saying, "Why are you writing bad stories about my friends?"

"Have you read it?" I asked.

"No," said Zoe.

I gave her a book, the next day she came up to me and said, "What you wrote may be true, but why do you have to put everybody's dirty laundry out."

The Cup dragged on, and the vibes got worse. The wanted posters were everywhere; the effect they had on the Cup and me was what Watson intended. I was isolated in a climate of hostility and danger.

WANTED:

For Crimes Against Cannabis
and the people who love it.

(WARNING: Be aware, Joseph R Pietri can not be trusted and is a snitch who has co-operated with police authorities in the past to get out of his own legal problems... and he makes lousy hash)

The poster put up by David Watson at the 19th Cannabis Cup in 2006.

In fact it appeared that Watson had handed them out to everyone who had a booth, but not everyone put them up. It would take a lot more than a Gorgeous George look-alike and a few angry hippies to rattle the King of Nepal.

DNA Genetics threw a large party, bragged that it cost them 80,000 Euros, and won a Cup for their crappy schwagg, Martian Mean Green. I guess when the fix is in you get a Cup no matter what.

Near the end of the event I met with Ed Rosenthal who told me, "You are living proof that the cannabis scene is non-violent." So, my murder or violence towards me had been discussed, and it was voted down?

Ed Rosenthal

When I got back home to Oregon, I started to look into David Watson some more. What I uncovered was alarming, and the more I researched, the more disturbed I became. Turns out, when Watson said I "blew" his "cover," it had a much deeper meaning than I realized at the time.

CHAPTER 2

A Road Less Traveled

My interest in a new way of hash making had its first inklings when I was at the 2002 Toker's Bowl in Vancouver and shared a booth with Mark Richardson aka "Bubbleman." I spent three days watching him sell bubblebags, and I tasted many of the samples. The first thing I noticed was the lack of flavor, aroma, and high associated with fine hashish. Also the hashish was often green, which meant it had been contaminated with plant matter. The buds the hash was made from were stronger than the final product.

This seemed improbable because after you separate the resin glands, the resultant hashish should be at least ten times stronger than the bud it came from. If you used thirty grams of bud to make hashish, you should end up with three grams of resin concentrate, and twenty-seven grams of plant matter left over. In Nepal it took ten kilos of cannabis to make a kilo of hashish. The bubble bags were being made in Nepal, an original source country famed for its hand-pressed hashish.

The technique made me curious, and I started studying the information on making hashish then being taught in grow books. One that I picked up was Robert Clarke's 1998 book, *Hashish!* On page 334 he wrote about water extraction: "In the early 1980s, Sadu Sam, a committed California *Cannabis* enthusiast, developed a water extraction technique." Clarke also promoted "Holland's

High-Tech Hashish," featuring a new Dutch product, the Pollinator, "an automated resin-collector." The book was put out by Red Eye Press, which, since the late 1970s, had published a well-known grow book, *Marijuana Grower's Guide* by Mel Frank. I also noticed in Clarke's book references to smugglers I had known in the 1970s, and felt that the book was basically a lot of second- and third-hand information. I dismissed the book.

Then at Christmas 2004, I was given copies of Jason King's *The Cannabible 1&2* (Clarke wrote the Foreword to *The Cannabible 1*), and

though the pictures were wonderful, I took exception to what I read in the *Cannabible 2*'s chapter on "Water Hash." Again, the story of Sadu Sam was told, but added was: "In his [Sadu Sam] literature he thanks Nevil [Schoenmakers] the King of Cannabis Castle for discovering this technique. Legend has it that an unnamed American gave the idea to Nevil."

I wondered who that unnamed American was, probably some old smuggler like me who had seen this technique used in Pakistan or Afghanistan. I had first seen a water separation method used in Peshawar, Pakistan around 1973. They were Danish smugglers, who no doubt learned it from a local hash maker. Basically the plant material floats and the resins sink. This is a method/process of resin separation, and shouldn't be confused with water-pressed hashish which uses water, instead of oils or other substances, as a binder with dry sifted plant material and resin. I had smoked water-pressed hash in 1968 and 1969 in New York City, and enjoyed it immensely. I did have definite ideas on the subject.

I contacted King through email and told him what I thought and that he'd obviously hadn't spoken to any old-time smugglers. He didn't reply, but I soon received an email from someone called, "Sam Skunkman." I told him my story of seeing a water method in Asia in the '70s. His comment to me, I'll always remember: "Are those guys still alive?"

I then came across an advertisement for the XTR 1000 (which I first thought was another rip-off), and found a site on the Internet, icecold.org, which in 1997 revealed a device, the XTR 420, which used a patented "Ice Water Method, [to] automate the plant resin extraction process." I called the 800 number and talked directly with the machine's inventor Reinhard Delp. He said his method was completely different from the traditional hash-making methods. He didn't grind the material, he used fresh buds or plant matter, and he used ice water.

I made arrangements to visit Delp in northern California, and watched him whip up a batch. In just a little time I was smoking the finest hashish I had ever seen in over forty years of being in the business, and soon found myself on a very interesting path – trying to fathom the truth of the matter, and most difficult, speaking up, trying to discuss the subject. Cannabis, after all, was still illegal, and there were many different tales being told.

For some it's

MILLENNIUM NEWS !

FOR THOUSANDS OF YEARS mankind has benefitted from the natural abundance of fragrant plants, extracting essential oils and fragrant resins, using these valuable substances for pleasure and medicine.

TODAY, when artificial flavors and synthetic drugs are dominating, more and more people choose their own alternative way of well being and healing, claiming total authority over their body, a right that is violently attacked by special interest laws, dispite written constitutional guarantees.

Based on the new ice-water method, the X-TRACTOR series offers a variety of products from exclusive connoisseur equipment to high volume farm machinery

* Traditionally fragrant resins were extracted for preservation and commerce in the high mountains where the seasonal cold allows a dry sifting.

* The new ice water method uses clean cold water and ice as the extraction environment, resulting in high quality resins at high quantities, since the plantmaterial stays intact and fibrous particles are also separated.

* Even fresh plant material can be processed.

The method was developed for a member of the Galia plant family, known to the Native Americans as a healing plant. The process is part of a complete closed-circle method to separate valuable plant components.
(Aromatherapy, Medicine, Cosmetics, Food etc., US pat. pend.).
Everything is reused - nothing wasted,- without chemical solvents - except clean cold water

POLLINATOR

Cornelis Troostraat 37, Postbus 76175, 1070 ED, Amsterdam, Nederland.
Ph: 31 20 4708889 Fax: 31 20 4715242
e-mail Greenfo@euronet.nl web: www.Amsterdampage.com

We wish you Happy Holidays - on ice   Peace   ETT, Zlin, Czech Rep.

Product flyer Delp.made for 1997 Cannabis Cup

CHAPTER 3

A Toke of Contention

In 1997 inventor and long-time cannabis grower Reinhard Delp introduced his Ice Water Method to the world in Amsterdam at the 10th *High Times* Cannabis Cup, and it was off to the races. Delp's novel discovery appears to have become the most copied and ripped-off formula in cannabis history.

During the Cup, Delp had offers from "an English Pharmaceutical outfit" that promised him the world for an exclusive license of his patent-pending method. He also performed a comparison test with a local hash-making machine, Mila Jansen's Pollinator. (A machine I have owned and used.) Delp's process won hands down for quantity and quality. But he refused the "exclusive" and insisted on immediate use for everybody.

At the end of the Cup, HortaPharm, a Dutch cannabis company founded by David Watson and Robert Clarke set up a meeting with Delp where Clarke said, "We can't publish that." And when asked why, responded, "The people can't handle it, it is too strong." Reinhard told Clarke that he was full of it, and they fell out. Delp didn't want to play monopoly games; he had been a political radical in the sixties and felt that his invention was for everyone, not for just a few. The meeting happened at Bill Barth's place, a much liked, very outspoken fellow, who was unimpressed by Clarke at the meeting.

What happened next is amazing. It appears Clarke and others set out to "hijack" this new method.

In a *High Times* May 1998 article (the magazine regularly comes out four months ahead, so this would be around February '98) the cannabis world was introduced to Delp's new machine and his revolutionary new process, but *Delp wasn't mentioned at all*. His patented ice water method was "watered" down to a "cold-water bath," and customers are told that they could get a machine from Jansen's "Pollinator company" in Amsterdam.

The X-Tractor

The Pollinator company out of Amsterdam is now marketing the newest improvement in resin-collecting devices, called the X-TRACTOR. Traditionally, THC resin was collected by drying high-quality cannabis and then sifting it through progressively finer screens until only a powdery residue of resin glands was left. It was then heated and compressed into blocks of hashish.

This work was done by hand for generations. In recent years, however, machines have been developed to do a more efficient job in less time. Resembling common laundry dryers, these machines tumble the dried cannabis, shaking loose the resin glands, as well as small bits of plant matter, which are then filtered through fine screens and collected for processing into hash.

The system is more efficient and less time-consuming and labor-intensive than the old method. The X-TRACTOR utilizes the same basic principles, but instead of tumbling cannabis through air to dislodge the resin glands from the plant matter, it agitates it in a cold-water bath to achieve the same results.

THC resin is insoluble in water and is also heavier than water. This makes it possible to use the liquid as a medium for its removal from the plant. To use the X-TRACTOR, fill it with ice water and plant matter. When you agitate it, the water gets cloudy as resin breaks away. The resin then falls through the water, where it is funneled into a glass bottle after settling through screens that filter and separate it from any tiny bits of plant matter that may drift downwards.

The result is a bottle of water clouded with pure resin which can then be separated and dried, using a coffee filter. The dried resin is then ready for processing. What makes this system unique is that by using water as the medium of extraction, it can process either dried or fresh plant matter.

This makes it much more efficient since, if fresh cannabis is used, much less resin is lost during drying, when many glands would be knocked off due to handling, etc. Also, because THC resin is an oil, it gets less viscous as the temperature falls. Using cold water "hardens" the glands and softens the plant matter, making their separation easier. This means more resin can be collected from the same amount of fresh or dried cannabis than if done the old way.

The X-TRACTOR can also be used to extract essential oils and fragrant resins from other plant species for use in aromatherapy, medicine, cosmetics and foodstuffs. The device comes in several sizes, for the personal connoisseur or the high-volume commercial producer, and can be purchased by writing, calling, or visiting the company's Web site.

The Pollinator company can be reached at: Cornelis Troostraat 37, Postbus 76175, 1070 ED, Amsterdam, NETHELANDS; phone (011) 31 20 470-3889; Web site: www.Amsterdampage.com.

None of the manufacturers or distributors mentioned in this column advocate the use of their products for the cultivation of illegal substances. If you contact them, do not discuss the cultivation of illegal substances in any way. These are not paid advertisements.

THE X-TRACTOR IS A MORE EFFICIENT, LESS TIME-CONSUMING METHOD OF HASH MAKING.

Then Clarke's book, *Hashish!*, was printed in May 1998, where he lays the whole water-extraction method as being "developed" by Sadu Sam. At the end of the section, Clarke denigrates the method: "the wet resin paste must be heated and pressed to remove the water. If all water is not removed, the piece must be consumed immediately, or it will spoil. Also some of the varietal aromas and flavors wash away." Clarke then talks about a "tool for wet-sieving Cannabis resins": the Baba Bob's Aqua-X-Tractor, which was never commercially available, and appears to be Clarke's invention. Both Sadu Sam and Baba Bob use ground-up dried material, which is fundamentally different from Delp's X-Tractor.

Matter of fact, Clarke didn't mention Delp's machine at all in the text, even though he had seen the machine and its method six months earlier. But he may have mentioned Delp's machine in the captions for Water Extraction: "With the X-Tractor or with Sadu Sam's, all that is needed are jars, plates, and coffee filters." Delp's X-Tractor does use coffee filters, and according to Clarke the Baba Bob's Aqua-X-Tractor used nylon or polyethylene sieve cloth.

According to an email from Clarke's publisher, James Goodwin, it would have been absolutely impossible for Clarke to mention Delp's product and/or method. In a 1999 letter to Delp, Goodwin stated: "The editor, Mel Frank, began editing Rob's manuscript in November of 1994. Sadu Sam's Secret and Baba Bob's Aqua-X-Tractor were in the original manuscript as was the accompanying artwork – this is two to three years before your introduction of Xtractor [sic] in November, 1997," and "As publisher, and for the editor Mel Frank, I can assure you that Rob Clarke added nothing new to the text after 1995."

Does that mean that Clarke was psychic and just happened upon the same name used by Delp? I also find it interesting that there are books in the *Hashish!* bibliography dated 1996 and 1998. Plus the fact that Mr. Goodwin speaks of Mel Frank in the third person, since Goodwin and Frank *are* the same person. But then there seems to be several folks that are *also known as* someone else in this tale.

Reinhard Delp

Jansen later applied for and received a government grant to develop her own machine: the Ice-O-Lator. Amazingly, Jansen sold her machine with the instructions that were copied directly from the XTR 420. "Sam Skunkman" in an email to Delp stated: "I did help Mila and Bubbleman with development of their products."

Mila Jansen

Jansen, as have many involved in this story, has been quoted, saying different things at different times, but her basic line is that Delp's machines didn't work, "they broke down a lot," so she "invented" a new machine.

There were times Jansen would recognize her contract with Delp, and pay money to an investor in the X-Tractor, but she never paid Delp anything, nothing for his X-Tractors, and nothing for the Ice-O-Lator either. Even though her contract stated quite plainly: "This contract is a licensing for distribution. It refers to equipment using the Ice Watter Method of separating fragrant plants." The contract specifically didn't license the XTR 420, but any equipment using Delp's "Ice Water Method."

Delp states that he had informed Jansen in 1997 about using a bucket and mixer for the process, as he had used that technique during the years he had spent in development. His X-Tractor apparatus he felt was easier to use, more elegant than a bucket and demonstrated the process better. Delp's "aha" moment had come during a winter at his California home in the early 1990s, when he put raw cannabis into a bucketful of snow.

In 1998, Delp went back to Amsterdam to confront Jansen. He found her demonstrating *her* Ice-O-Lator at the '98 Cup. When Delp reminded Jansen of their contract, she asked him if he had seen Robert Clarke's new book, *Hashish!*, implying that she didn't have to pay, because Delp's "discovery" was nothing but old news.

Were the actions by Clarke and Jansen designed to dilute Delp's patent claims and hijack his method? And who was Sadu Sam? Was he related to Sam Skunkman?

AMSTERDAM   NOV. 30, 1997
CONTRACT   BETWEEN:
REINHARD C. DELP , LAYTONVILLE , CA , USA.
AND
MILA M. JANSEN, ~~CALIFORNIA~~ AND OR POLLINATOR
COMPANY - GREENFINGERS , DOS # 33266193

THIS CONTRACT IS A LICENSING FOR DISTRIBUTION.
IT REFERS TO EQUIPMENT - USING THE ICE-WATER
METHOD OF SEPERATING FRAGRANT PLANTS (US PAT. PEN)

REINHARD C. DELP - OWNER OF THE PAT. PEND.
LICENSES MILA M. JANSEN AND OR POLLINATOR
COMP. FOR WORLD WIDE DISTRIBUTION OF ABOVE
DESCRIBED EQUIPMENT.
FOR THE EUROPEAN COMMUNITY THOSE RIGHTS
ARE EXCLUSIVE. THOSE RIGHTS ARE NOT
TRANSFERABLE AND CEASE IF NO DISTRIBUTION
TAKES PLACE ,

MILA M. JANSEN IN RETURN PAYS
REINHARD C. DELP 10 (TEN)% OF THE
WHOLESALE PRICE OF ABOVE DESCRIBED
EQUIPMENT AS A LICENSING FEE.

        A'DAM   NOV. 30, 97

    REINHARD C DELP   MILA M. JANSEN
                                 (Pollinator Comp.)

Delp and Jansen's 1997 contract.

world class seeds

-SAM THE SKUNKMAN'S-

 CULTIVATORS CHOICE

UNIT #70   N.2. XDLK 33
1012 PV AMSTERDAM
           HOLLAND

prices effective Nov. 1, 1985

SKUNK #1   f1 per seed

ALL OTHER VARIETIES   f2 per seed

MINIMUM ORDER f50
Use enclosed order form

Price does not reflect quality of seed variety
but merely supply and demand

PRICES ARE SUBJECT TO CHANGE

ALL TRANSACTIONS ARE CASH ONLY
PLEASE ENCLOSE PAYMENT WITH ORDER
ALL ORDERS SHIPPED PROMPTLY·WE PAY SHIPPING CHARGES
SEEDS SHIPPED WITHIN HOLLAND ONLY·CATALOGS ANYWHERE
OFFER VOID WHERE PROHIBITED BY LAW

WE SUGGEST MINIMUM OF 20 SEEDS OF ANY 1 VARIETY
10% DISCOUNT ON ORDERS OF f1000 OR MORE

For additional copies of this catalog, include
stamped, self addressed envelope with request
outside of Holland, include US$1·° for catalog
COLOR CATALOG WITH DETAILED
INFORMATION AVAILABLE SOON

CULTIVATOR'S CHOICE
CATALOG # 4   FALL 1985

CULTIVATORS CHOICE, CREATORS OF SKUNK SEEDS,
HIGH BREED AND SELECT SEEDS IS THE WORLDS
LEADING EXPLORER, IMPORTER, CULTIVATOR, BREEDER
AND RESEARCHER OF SELECT, EXOTIC, PEDIGREED
CANNABIS SEED.

CULTIVATORS CHOICE OFFERS THE FINEST OF:
* PURE, TRUE BREEDING VARIETIES
* THE ULTIMATE N. F₁ HYBRIDS
* SUPERIOR, IMPORTED SEED FROM THE WORLD OVER

CULTIVATORS CHOICE IS PROUD TO OFFER THESE INCREDIBLE
SEEDS TO THOSE WHO CAN TRULY APPRECIATE THEM

* NOTE: THESE SEEDS ARE NOT AN ACCIDENTAL BY PRODUCT
OF COMMERCIAL CANNABIS PRODUCTION. THEY ARE FROM
CONSCIOUSLY CHOSEN SEED STRAINS, CAREFULLY
CULTIVATED AND SCIENTIFICALLY POLLINATED · THE
ENTIRE MOTIVATION IS TO PRODUCE VIGOROUS, HEALTHY
SEEDS OF THE HIGHEST QUALITY AND PURITY.

* WARNING: GROWING CANNABIS MAY NOT BE LEGAL IN
YOUR AREA · CHECK YOUR LOCAL LAWS.

* CULTIVATORS CHOICE IS ALWAYS LOOKING FOR NEW
SEED STRAINS, ESPECIALLY EXOTIC IMPORTED SEED
PLEASE CONTACT CULTIVATORS CHOICE WITH INFORMATION.

* CULTIVATION CONSULTATION AVAILABLE *

Chapter 4

Smells Like Skunk

Steve Hager joined *High Times* in 1986, and first visited the Netherlands in 1987 to write an article titled "The King of Cannabis." The article described how an Australian, Nevil Schoenmakers, established a mail-order seed company in Holland.

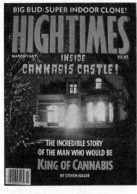

In June 2002 before the 15th Cannabis Cup, Hager wrote: "While working on the article ['King of Cannabis'], I met the founders of Cultivators Choice, an almost defunct American cannabis-seed company. They told me about the spectacular California harvest festivals of the '70s. That's when I got the idea of holding a cannabis harvest festival in Amsterdam."

Later in a 2005 book, in an piece about the 2002 Cup, Hager again recounted history: "While in Amsterdam, I met the founders of the Sacred Seed Company, an underground, California-based company that provided essential genetics to Nevil. These two Americans told me about harvest festivals that had been held in California before the CAMP [Campaign Against Marijuana Planting] clampdown of the '80s. Skunk #1, their favorite strain, had apparently won many prizes.

"Since there were already three seed companies operating in Holland, it seemed like a no-brainer – why not hold a harvest festival in Holland like the ones that had taken place in the late '70s in California?"

In a 2014 online posting at Abakus Magazine, Hager gives us more data and some changes: "I went off to Holland to meet Nevil and was waylaid by Sam the Skunkman and Robert Clarke… They wanted to give me their spin on Nevil's operation, and the quality of Dutch homegrown versus Cali…. Truth is, Sam had no idea I'd be inventing the Cannabis Cup later that year, as I didn't get the idea until I was on the plane home…. When I returned to Holland for the first Cannabis Cup months later, Sam was there to meet me."

In 1986 when he joined *High Times,* Hager had no deep background in cannabis; he was not a dealer, smuggler, or a grower. He was a journalist, a newbie on the scene. And only knew what folks told him. Sam the Skunkman and Clarke both smoked up a storm, had trusted contacts and talked a great line of patter. Ed Rosenthal knew them, and he had been reporting from the Amsterdam scene in the late '70s for *High Times* and other magazines.

To his credit Hager did clean up the cocaine vibe that had taken over the magazine after Tom Forçade passed. From the late '70s until Hager took over, cocaine had appeared to have replaced cannabis in *High Times,* with pink Peruvian fish flake making the centerfold.

I am sure that before, during and after Hager, undercover agents have become embedded into *High Times*; they are sheep-dipped, i.e. going undercover using *High Times* credentials. Who facilitates this, and who is aware is unknown. Whether it is coordinated is also unknown, but the intelligence gathering capabilities are there, nor is it the first time that intelligence agencies have used media as a front.

The "old school" ways of cannabis imports were coming to an end by the time Hager took over in 1986, and by 1990 the glory years of cannabis were over. Ronald Reagan had shut down much of the cannabis imports and had busted out the "good old boy" marijuana syndicates, some that had been in operation since the 1930s.

So there were very few left to advise or work with Hager; they were either in prison, left with nothing, or disappeared into the woodwork. His naiveté was evident and most likely used against him. He had no Drug War experience. In other words he did not know what the police looked and smelled like.

Report from Europe:

Grass, Coke Still Cheap and Plentiful in Amsterdam

A good place to party: houseboat on Amsterdam canal.

by Ed Rosenthal

Amsterdam is an international city. It's a magnet for young people from all of Europe as well as former Dutch colonies in Asia, Africa and the West Indies. In marked contrast to the homogeneous provincial cultures found in other European cities (and most American ones), everyone speaks several languages—including French, Spanish and German—and you can assume that all urban Dutch speak English.

Amsterdam is a city of joy. Its people are into good times and have a lightness and genuine friendliness found in few other places. The city is an entertainment and tourist center comparable to San Francisco, with an inordinate number of restaurants, night clubs, discos, concert and recital halls, museums and other cultural trimmings. It appeals to everyone because it has so much to offer. The streets of Amsterdam are filled with longhairs. There are free outdoor concerts during the summer, and dope smoking is an accepted way of life. It is not unusual to see people smoking outdoors and, since the Provo riots of the '60s, there is no fear of repression from the cops, who act in a very nonhostile, nonthreatening manner.

Cannabis and cocaine (it always snows in Amsterdam) are plentiful and inexpensive, since they come off the freighters that dock in Rotterdam, an hour's train ride away. Dealing takes place in clubs and restaurants as well as the more usual private places.

The heads in Europe are very different from those in the U.S. The first thing one notices is that they smoke hash in joints mixed with tobacco. They tend to chuckle at the crazy American with his or her hash pipe. Virtually all adults smoke tobacco, and there is much less emphasis on health, physical fitness and natural foods. Dopers are more disaffected from society, and they do not seem as integrated into the cultural mainstream as they are in the U.S.; a smaller proportion of the society seems to have been affected by the culture.

Among the most exciting places in Amsterdam are two clubs, the Milky Way and the Cosmos. The Milky Way is housed in a building behind the opera house, right off a main square in the entertainment section. At the Milky Way you need a membership that is available for a one- or three-month period. The entrance fee is about $3. The club houses a coffeehouse-snack bar-smoking room, a music and light-theater room with stage and dance floor, an open-space room that is used for workshops, classes and projects and which doubles as a crafts salesroom, and a bakery where, among other treats, they make space balls and space cakes. On the second level there is a music recital hall, intimate coffeehouse and a movie theater.

Rosenthal article promoting drug tourism to Holland in *Stone Age*, Winter,1978

One thing Reagan did after taking office in 1981 was allow the police to get high and even sell loads, as a way to infiltrate the old-school marijuana syndicates. As Reagan shut down imports, and cannabis products became scarce, people who took chances and worked outside of their personal connections were busted as well. Drivers busted with loads made controlled deliveries to everyone they had ever delivered to. It was wholesale round-up time. Slowly but surely the big syndicates were shut down, and with war brewing in Afghanistan, the "hippie trail" and the old-school smuggling was soon only a fond memory. Growing one's own became more and more the thing.

Skunkman and Clarke had impressed Hager with their tales. And in 1988 the first Cannabis Cup was held, and lo and behold, Cultivators Choice won for Skunk #1.

Later funny things started to happen around Amsterdam; many of Skunkman's competitors were being busted, including growers to whom he had sold seeds. Skunkman's own warehouse grows were busted as well, but he remained untouched. He took his money to Luxembourg and returned to go on, while everyone else went to jail. Even though all his workers ratted him out, he remained unscathed.

Something definitely smelled like skunk.

CHAPTER 5

Operation Green Merchant

Peter Gorman, a former editor of *High Times,* once said that anyone stupid enough to order seeds from the magazine deserved to busted.

How many people have been compromised over the years by covert police stings?

Gorman wrote in the May '91 *High Times* an update about Operation Green Merchant: "Marijuana is illegal today only because the big boys haven't yet seen their way clear to corner the market once it does become legal. But you can bet they are working on that; marijuana is just too valuable to be kept off the market forever. It's just a question of working out the details – among which is ridding the marketplace of as many independent  Peter Gorman growers and as much information as possible. That part of the plan went into effect on Black Thursday – October 26, 1989."

By the end of 1991, the operation had arrested 1,262 people, shut down 977 indoor grows, and confiscated $17.5 million in assets. Dozens served 4- to 15-year prison terms, many with mandatory sentences that did not allow for any reduction.

Operation Green Merchant began in 1987, the brainchild of DEA agent, Jim Stewart. The targets were *High Times, Sinsemilla Tips,* Nevil Schoenmakers, and the blossoming indoor-grow industry. *Sinsemilla Tips,* a respected grow magazine was put out of business.

In 1989, raids were conducted in forty-six states on grow shops and wholesalers. After the dust settled the only big fish left was *High Times.*

According to Jeff Edwards, in the Winter 2004 issue of *Hydroponic Retailing In the USA*: "The DEA in the late 1980's believed that *High Times* magazine, pot seed merchants, indoor pot growers, pot journalists and hydroponics equipment manufacturers were a criminal conspiracy worthy of a nationwide takedown."

Operation Green Merchant worked many angles. In Hawaii the Feds opened a grow store in Kona, partied, smoked and got to know some growers. They offered growers a deal: we will give you seeds, nutrients, whatever you need. You grow the product, and bring it here, where we will ship it to your people. You collect the money and pay us a share.

Only a few went for the deal at first. It went super smooth; all the packages arriving safely, monies paid, and a share given to the grow shop. The following year many more jumped on board, and folks were busted from Kona to Brooklyn. You can only imagine the numbers, hundreds of folks lost everything, many went to prison. Busted were companies who had advertised in *High Times* or *Sinsemilla Tips*.

It is an old police trick, set up a front and get the "criminals" to come to you, and you infiltrate the scene, get information, take names and track the dynamics. But there also may be another rationale at work: control/influence over the international marijuana trade.

"Hippies" had taken over much of the cannabis trade, spiriting it away from the forces in the shadows (criminal gangs, intelligence agencies) and, maybe, "they" wanted it back. According to the UN 2009 Drug Report: The cannabis market is the largest illicit drug market in terms of global spread of cultivation, volume of production and number of consumers. The 2005 UN report put a market value on the worldwide marijuana trade at 141.8 billion dollars a year, a hefty sum. And there are those who would like to curtail the cultural effects of marijuana.

Tom Alexander, the Editor *Sinsemilla Tips*, the most popular grow magazine at the time, was a target of Operation Green Merchant. After his arrest, due to family pressure Alexander elected to retire from publishing, and a major source for true cannabis growing techniques was lost to the drug war.

Tom Alexander

From a December '90 *High Times* article by Gorman, "Recalling the raid, part of Operation Green Merchant, Alexander explained: 'They seized strip irrigation, lights and other items. What they basically did was arrest the merchandise. They never arrested me or charged me with anything.

"'They said that since I had a store which supposedly sold marijuana growing equipment it constituted a criminal conspiracy. If the fuckers had a criminal conspiracy case they would have come and charged me, but they didn't. Nonetheless, for two months they were hanging that over my head.'

"'There was no agreement made whatsoever in relation to *Tips*. No type of overt pressure or coercion was used; no plea of any sort that I stop *Tips*. The only agreement I made was that I wouldn't contest them stealing my merchandise if they would just get off my back. Fighting the civil forfeiture of the store's merchandise was going to cost $20,000. I looked at those numbers and decided it wasn't worth it. I had wanted to sell the store for two years by that time. Instead of selling it, I had it stolen (by the government). They used the law as a tool of extortion. It wasn't worth my remaining assets to fight these assholes.'

"Alexander added that 'after 10 and-a-half years *Tips* will be dead. It's no longer financially viable. If it was, I'd still be doing it.'"

In 1990, Nevil Schoenmakers, former owner of The Seed Bank became the target of Operation Green Merchant, some said because of the press he had received from *High Times*.

Gorman wrote about the bust in the October '90 issue of *High Times*: "Nevil Martin Schoenmakers, operator of Holland's Seed Bank, was arrested in Australia on July 24, at the request of the U.S. government. At press time, extradition proceedings were underway to

Nevil Schoenmakers

27

transport Schoenmakers to Federal court in New Orleans, where he will face charges of violating the Controlled Substances Act.

"The 44-count indictment alleges that Schoenmakers, 'in concert with at least five other persons,' knowingly distributed, through the U.S. Postal Service, a total of 1,921 seeds to DEA agents and marijuana growers in the New Orleans area from 1985 to 1990. The indictment also alleges that Schoenmakers, an Australian native who makes his home in Holland, 'did knowingly ... manufacture (grow) more than 1,000 marijuana plants, a Schedule 1 drug controlled substance.' If convicted on all counts, Schoenmakers (as well as a second, unnamed 'co-conspirator') faces a possible life sentence.

"Schoenmakers' indictment is closely tied to the ongoing grand jury investigation of *High Times* being conducted by U.S. District Attorney John Volz. The government has been seeking to determine whether or not conspiracy charges can be brought against the magazine for allowing advertisers to offer products through the mail which may later have been used in indoor-growing operations in the New Orleans area."

It came out later that Schoenmakers' lawyer in court records had noted that the police had a dossier on his client, as well as everyone who was anyone in the Dutch scene. These reports had been compiled by informants in Amsterdam.

Cannabis Culture, October '05: "Using gardening equipment ads in *High Times* as their roadmap, undercover DEA agents visited hydroponics stores and contacted hydroponics wholesalers.... Congress started passing laws in 1985 that criminalized otherwise legal products if they were 'intended for illegal use.'"

So, in 1985 the DEA gets its marching orders, the Cannabis Cup began in 1988, and then Operation Green Merchant's first bust is October 1989. Was the Cannabis Cup a target, or more sinister, had it been used as part of Operation of Green Merchant?

How best for law enforcement and the DEA to get information on growers? Every top grower in the world goes to Amsterdam for the Cannabis Cup – a bonanza of data for law enforcement agencies around the globe!

One wonders when or if the folks at *High Times* realized that?

CHAPTER 6

Amsterdam

In the 1970s there was very little if any marijuana available in Holland; in Europe in general it has always been a hashish-mixed-with-tobacco scene.

Why bother with ganja when the hash is ten times stronger and very cheap. Amsterdam had always been the cheapest place to buy hashish in Europe; in the late '60s you could buy hash in Holland, dip it in chocolate and mail it home in a Dutch box of chocolates. It was easy and cheap back then.

I had a false bottom suitcase factory in Bombay, and was sending runners to Australia and Canada because the price was high, never to Amsterdam because of the low price.

It was very easy to get into Europe in those days and back packers and suitcase runners made their way to Amsterdam. It was safe and easy and if you got caught, it was a short time in jail with good food, beer and even hash to smoke, and you got a ticket home.

Author packing hash for shipment, Nepal 1970s.

Amsterdam and London became the crossroads to Asia with bus overland travel as far as Nepal. The big market in those days was London. The highest prices and biggest selection of hashish and weed were available in London, not Amsterdam, but you could get five years in the nick in London; in Amsterdam less than six months.

Wernard
Bruining

Wernard Bruining is the grandfather of the Dutch coffee shop scene. In 1973 Bruining had the vision to open the coffee shop, Mellow Yellow. It had a house dealer who would handle small sales to customers. A lot of great hashish was sold there back in the day.

From Bruining's online autobiography: "Customers lined up in front of our house dealer at the bar, through the shop, 10-15 meters up the sidewalk. Our booming business inspired others to do the same, and to do it better! In 1975 Maarten Brusselers, an old house friend, opened up The Rusland, a few months later followed by Henk de Vries who opened his first Bulldog."

The police would look the other way; it enabled them to resell the hashish that was confiscated back to the coffee shops. Law Enforcement throughout Europe sold their confiscated cannabis stock to Dutch Police, who in turn would move it through the coffee shops to tourists. As the coffee shop scene grew, the police even setup a clearing warehouse, where you could buy the confiscated stock; then they even opened their own coffee shops. It became big business.

After fire took out the Mellow Yellow in 1978, Bruining went on a vacation to the States. While there he met folks that were growing sinsemilla marijuana. At that time the marijuana imported or grown in Holland wasn't very good, and Wernard brought some Americans back with him to Holland to remedy that.

Among them was Old Ed Holloway from Oregon. Old Ed brought with him high-potency marijuana seeds and the sinsemilla technique. He lived with Bruining for five years, and helped him and his associates, known as the "Green Team," raise Holland's first sinsemilla crop in 1979 in a plastic greenhouse in Amsterdam.

Old Ed

30

The Green Team bought a small farm in 1980, and began to grow sinsemilla outdoors. In 1981 Wernard and a friend started the Lowland Seed Company, the first cannabis seed company in Europe.

What happened next still reverberates today. From Bruining's autobiography: "Slowly our production grew up to a couple of hundred kilos a year. The success of the Green Team attracted more and more 'associates' who had their own business opinions. In 1984 the Green Team felt we needed some extra input so we send tickets to two Americans, inviting them to come over to Amsterdam for a chat, a guy called the Skunkman and Ed Rosenthal, the famous writer of 'how to grow sinsemilla' books. The Skunkman brought his Skunk seeds that gave sensational results when grown under lights or in greenhouses. Coffee shop customers went wild when the first Skunk became available. That's why the Skunkman was chosen by the majority of the Green Team, while I voted for Ed Rosenthal and his publicity potential. The Green Team planned to grow in a couple of big greenhouses, I figured I did not came to this planet to become a large scale illegal sinsemilla grower, so I abandoned the Green Team and Old Ed went back to the States.

"That same year, I started a company of my own called Positronics. I designed a reflector and at the end of a cable a remote ballast and asked a friend of mine to assemble my light systems in a shed in the back of my garden. Positronics was the first grow shop in Europe and the business attracted a lot of people. In the beginning customers were mainly my friends. Later customers came from all over Holland, then from all over Europe and much later from all over the world. Positronics grew quickly to a company that employed 60 people, produced seeds, clones, lights, fertilizers, and sold everything needed for organic growing. We had a vegetarian restaurant and a newspaper called *Soft Secrets*. I hosted journalists on a weekly basis; they helped us to spread the message of home growing."

Bruining let Skunkman stay at a house his girlfriend had squatted in temporarily, but Bruining soon moved on, concentrating more on Positronics. He thought Skunkman was loud, and focused too much on money.

Mel Frank   Marijuana Man

CHAPTER 7

THE HORSE'S MOUTH

OriInally released on August 24th, 2006, and uploaded to You Tube on January 11, 2010:
"In an exclusive interview for Pot TV, Marijuana Man talks with the original pot author Mel Frank. Starting in the earliest days of *Rolling Stone* and *High Times*, his collaboration with Ed Rosenthal and *The Marijuana Grower's Guides* vaulted him to ganja guru status."

Marijuana Man: So you were in and around the development of some of the most earliest hybrids with, you know, Northern California?

Mel Frank: That was something that came later. I have a friend who was in California at that time. He was very good breeder, very conscientious and he was working on Haze, which was already something that he got from other growers, but he consistently grew it, trying to get it to be the best it could be, and also Skunk #1. So, I think it was in '83 or '84 he got busted for the second time, he was a married man with two kids – two young kids – and needed to leave the country. He said he just couldn't live here anymore, he couldn't do what he did, what was grow dope, so he moved to Amsterdam, and needed a way to get started there, and he came by and asked me if I would give him a couple of pure strains, you know good stuff. I gave him Durbin Poison, which I thought was one of the best things I ever did and Afghani #1. He took Skunk #1, Afghani #1, Haze and Durbin Poison to Amsterdam which basically started the entire seed breeding thing.

Marijuana Man: It absolutely did.

SKUNK *red hair*

ZADEN ☆ 10 HANDGESELECTEERDE

12.⁹⁰

Sinsemilla Fanclub/Positronics
P.b. 51200-1007 EE AMSTERDAM - 020-797790

CHAPTER 8

What's Going On?

Now, things start to get really interesting ... and even more squishy. By squishy, I mean there are lots of differing stories, contested "facts," and folks using many names, but after all we are dealing with activities surrounding contraband. A contraband that is an emerging industry. A milieu of narcs, smugglers, middlemen, dealers, growers: energetic entrepreneurs. Outlaws who can be busted by the man. But a basic narrative can be teased from people's words and printed sources. After time it does get clearer.

A slew of books has come out on the cannabis scene, especially the last few years, many repeating similar stories. A few acknowledge that there are differences of history, but most do not.

So far, the Ice Water Method controversy hasn't been broached in any book except mine, *King of Nepal – Ice Wars Edition*. Reinhard Delp's patent and invention have been completely ignored by most books and magazine articles. I have written pieces for *Skunk* and *Treating Yourself* magazines, which engendered discussions on several cannabis forums. I have posted on some forums myself: receiving scorn, ridicule and denials. I have been called a rat, and banned from forums.

There have also been some very interesting items in the Dutch press, and even discussions by Dutch politicians, but the controversy smolders.

Let's peruse some of the written record.

From the 1999 book, *Cannabis Culture* by Patrick Mathews:

> One figure who has stayed out of the limelight is the American named "Skunk Sam" who brought seeds of this variety to Holland, collaborated for a time with Ben Dronkers of Sensi·Seeds, and has since disappeared from view. Skunk is so famous that it's become a generic term for modern high-potency weed.

From the 2012 book, *Super Charged* by Jim Rendon:

Most grow guides have sections devoted to breeding. [Mel]Frank and [Ed] Rosenthal's *Marijuana Grower's Guide* is no exception. Almost as soon as Frank began growing marijuana he began amassing a vast collection of seeds and breeding. In the 1970s Frank was getting seeds from Afghanistan, very pungent skunky weed, and some Durban Poison from South Africa, useful because of its fast maturation time. Frank, like most breeders, wanted to select the most potent plants to breed, but back then there were no labs set up to test for THC levels. So he had to get creative. Frank smoked his own marijuana and had his own impressions of the potency but he wanted a larger sample. He gave his friends numbered joints containing different strains of marijuana and asked them to write up a little report after they smoked each one. He asked them to be as regimented as possible about it – smoke at the same time each day and note how long the high lasts (which he figured was a good indicator of how potent the strain was). But it didn't always work out so well. "One woman wrote, 'well it was a really shitty day and the dog peed in the bed' – This is not a diary," Frank says, still sounding a little annoyed decades later. "I want to know about the dope."

In 1976 Frank and Rosenthal began to breed on a much larger scale. They bought a house in the Oakland hills with a small shed out back. They put in as many windows with frosted glass as they could and covered the inside with reflective material. As we talk, Frank pulls out a stack of yellowing paper-notes from his early years of breeding in Oakland in the late 1970s. Unlike many breeders at the time, Frank kept copious notes despite the risk. He felt that if he was ever put on trial, a jury in liberal-minded Oakland would not convict him since his work was geared towards research and seed production, not growing to sell for profit. He looks at his notes on an Afghani (an indica) and Nigerian crossed with a Hawaiian – both sativa dominant if not full sativas. "The hybrids were just so vigorous, they were so good in every aspect, they were wonderful," says Frank. Another list of seeds that he finds shows strains from Burma, Tibet, China, Thailand, Sumatra, Korea, Indonesia.

The pair had an incredible diversity of plants growing at any given time. "There was a South Indian that I grew that was so sweet that I just wanted to bite it every time I went in the greenhouse," Frank says. "There was the skunkiest skunk you'd ever had." (According to Frank, the skunk odor indicates an indicadominant strain.) The pair grew everywhere they could think of. "We grew in the attic, we had it in the windows and in the ground in the backyard and in pots. When I think of it, we were pretty outrageous," he says. "My sister came to visit and somebody came in and asked if there was any dope around. She said 'yeah, here,' and pulled some out from under the couch cushion. It was everywhere."

The seeds he and Rosenthal cultivated were the basis for the strains that he passed along to northern California growers and which they, in turn, began crossing as well, coming up with their own hybrids. As, it turns out, Frank's seeds were also used by the early seed companies in Amsterdam that shipped seeds all around the world and made it possible for just about anyone to grow their own marijuana.

In the early 1980s, Dave Watson, one of the pioneers of marijuana growing and breeding, who would go on to become a pivotal figure in the industry, was planning to move to Amsterdam and wanted some seed stock to take with him so he could start anew over there. Frank gave him Afghani #1 and Durban Poison. Watson added them to his collection which included Original Haze, Skunk #1, and Hindu Kush. The seeds in Watson's collection were an important part of the founding of the Amsterdam seed business.

From the 2012 book, *Smoke Signals* by Martin A. Lee:

A California-based cannabis advocate with a crusty sense of humor, Rosenthal was described by the *New York Times* as "the pothead's answer to Ann Landers, Judge Judy, Martha Stewart and the Burpee Garden Wizard all in one." Well known for his "Ask Ed" advice column in *High Times*, the unrepentant Yippie was instrumental in steering indoor growers toward high-intensity sodium lamps and other technological gadgetry that he flagged as a journalist. "I just give advice on how to cultivate a better garden. It's not my fault that marijuana, the plant that is my specialty, is illegal;" he explained. Rosenthal kept his readers abreast of new developments in the cannabis underground, such

as the Dutch "sea of green" gardens, wherein dozens of genetically identical plants grown from clones are crammed together
in greenhouses under a perpetual blaze of light, hot-wired to the
same nutrient regimen and forced to flower in lockstep. These
pampered plants had identical hairy calyxes with the same can-
nabinoid-terpenoid-flavonoid mix, the same resinous medicament.

Rosenthal and Dronkers were among the stoned cognoscen-
ti who gathered at the inaugural Cannabis Cup, hosted by *High
Times* in Amsterdam in 1987, underscoring once again that Holland was the place to be if you were into marijuana. What began
as a one-day contest evolved into a week-long celebration of all
things hemp, an annual psychoactive soirée that attracted thousands of ganja fans from around the world. There were speech-
es, strategy sessions, new product demonstrations, and lots of
pot parties, leading up to the climactic moment when the judg-
es reached their decision and crowned the year's best cannabis
strain, a verdict based on superb look, flavor, aroma, and quality
of the high. The winner of the first Cannabis Cup, the Oscars
of pot, was Skunk #1, an Afghan-sativa cross created by David
Watson, from Santa Cruz, California. A mercurial genius, Watson had been at the forefront of the great migration of American
talent to the Netherlands. Watson's award-winning weed was a
potent, adaptable hybrid and its genetics would be woven into
countless modern strains. (In the years ahead, pot prohibition-
ists misappropriated the term skunk and used it as a generic way
of referring to any strong reefer.) Watson "the Skunkman" and
his perspicacious business partner, Robert Connell Clarke, obtained a license from the Dutch government to pursue advanced
scientific research into cannabinoid botany. Their company,
HortaPharm, was not a commercial seed bank or grow operation. Formed in 1989, HortaPharm broke new ground in horticultural pharmacology.

Watson and Clarke isolated various phytocannabinoids and
terpenes in order to explore their medicinal potential. This dy-
namic duo took cannabis science to a whole other level. They
were the first to breed "chemovar" plants marijuana plants that
express just one cannabinoid. HortaPharm developed a THC
chemovar and a CBD chemovar – and that was just the beginning. They also created a seed library with hemp germ plasm

they had gathered from all over the world, a priceless collection that included old landrace cannabis strains threatened with extinction because of ecocidal U.S. drug-war policies.

From the 2012 book, *Heart of Dankness* by Mark Haskell Smith:

> Like all origination myths, there are several different versions of how the Dutch seed business began. All of the versions, interestingly, orbit around the introduction of a unique strain of cannabis called Haze into the world of underground botanists. One version has a Californian named David Watson – who goes by the nom d'weed Sam the Skunkman – bringing Haze genetics to Amsterdam and sharing them with several breeders, including Nevil [Schoenmaker]. Another interpretation has Nevil venturing to Santa Cruz, California, in the late '80s, where he encountered two local growers called the Haze Brothers. It was the brothers who introduced Nevil to the powerful Mexican sativa. Both Sam the Skunkman and Nevil have contentiously stuck by their stories in different interviews, although I have to say, just for the sake of argument, that there's no reason they both can't be right. Sam the Skunkman could've given Nevil seeds of Haze and Nevil still could've gotten other Haze seeds from the Haze Brothers.
>
> Naturally, Sam the Skunkman denies that Nevil got the real Haze, alternately claiming that he gave Nevil an inferior version of the plant or the Haze Brothers gave Nevil bad genetics. The truth – I dare I say it – *hazy*.

Now for an article that started many questions being raised. A Dutch monthly magazine, *HP/De Tijd,* published an investigative piece by Bas Barkman and Gert Hage on December 5, 1997. This article gave confirmation of a VPRO radio show that had aired on October 3rd. That show had sent a shock wave through Amsterdam's cannabis scene, which is still reverberating today. This is an English translation from the original Dutch:

Thanks to Uncle Sam

It was a lovely day, spring 1985, when a heavily built American landed at Schiphol airport. He wore glasses, his long blond hair kept together with an elastic band. Without problems he passed customs and shortly afterwards received a warm welcome from another equally heavily built American.

Seemingly nothing special, certainly not in the crowded arrivals area of an airport. No one could have known that the luggage of the ponytailed man contained a box full of seeds – cannabis seeds.

The box was the reason for Sam Selezny's trip to Holland. He was here by invitation from two pioneers in the weedgrowing industry. Two companions: Michael Taylor and Wernard Bruining, the owner of the first coffeeshop in Amsterdam. Although they already grew some nederwiet, the quality of it was not particularly special, the knowledge they possessed of growing wasn't extensive enough.

During that time in Holland, there were probably no more than three big growing sites, covering a total of a maximum of two thousand square meters. In coffeeshops Moroccan hash was still the most popular.

Sam Selezny, the super grower from the states, as Taylor had announced him to Bruining, would change this.

It proved to be true. Hardly three months after his arrival, the first harvest from Fat Sam's seeds could be smoked. The connoisseurs where excited, the wiet tasted good, with a "high" high.

Hardly anyone knew at that time, especially not in Holland, that Sam Selezny, who in Holland presented himself mainly under the name David Watson, was arrested on the 20th of March that same year in Santa Cruz, California.

It was nine years later in the summer of 1994, when Mario Lap, at that time working for the Dutch Alcohol and Drugs Institute, tapped Hedy D'Acona on the shoulder in Brussels.

"Hedy, can you tell me why you provided David Watson with a license (to grow)?" Lap asked the newly appointed MEP and former minister of Health. Lap had only just before that found out, to his utter astonishment, that Watson, whom he only knew by the name of Selezny, was granted a license to grow marijuana for scientific purposes.

Why on earth Watson, a man with what he had heard was a shady past in the states as illegal grower, a man who also had been detained and who certainly was not a scientist?

And why not the Academic Medical Center in Amsterdam, which had been after a license for years to research the medical workings of the plant?

MEP D'Acona didn't know.

The ministry itself couldn't provide Lap with any clearance on the license which had been granted on 16th of September 1994, signed by "plaatsvervangend" director general of health, Dr. RJ Samsom.

Lap: "I couldn't find out how it had happened. Very strange. A bit scary too."

In two big greenhouses in Rijsenhout, a village near Schiphol airport, the process was already under way to develop a cannabis plant with a high THC content, which in due course could be used as a basis for medicine. Or rather, it was on those terms that, after years of negotiating, the license was granted.

Three years, with limiting conditions; only chemical analytical research, not more than 10 grams of THC and a spotless administration.

The office and lab of HortaPharm are based in Schinkelhavenkade in Amsterdam. A little green building, a big window which in the evenings is covered with a steel sliding door. Inside it smells of fresh wiet. David Watson is on his guard. He wants to talk, but demands the final say on every sentence written about his firm. It is the end of September, and Watson is waiting for the decision on the renewal of his license. "I want to continue with my research," he says. "I cannot use any publicity which might be possibly disadvantageous to my business."

He is startled when he hears we know the location of his greenhouse. "There are millions worth of plants and apparatus; no one is allowed to know."

Hanging on the wall behind him are five licenses, granted by the DEA, a worldwide operating organization, whose task it is to fight drugs.

Watson didn't receive his longed-for renewal of his license.

The ministry announced at the end of September that, since the minister forbids the medical supply of cannabis, a license to grow cannabis is no longer in line with the health ministries' policies. Besides that, during repeated inspections of HortaPharm, it was found the Admin was not run according to the requirements.

The decision is definite, the two locations where HortaPharm is based have to close their doors. On 29 October [1997] the Ministry confirms their decision in writing to HortaPharm: The head officials of Justice in Haarlem and Amsterdam have been informed of the fact the license has now expired.

In Schinkelhavenkade however, it is business as usual, the director and only shareholder told us last Monday. He saw the decision of the minister in a different light. "There are people who want it that way," he said was the cryptic explanation, "but there are also people who want it in a different way."

From his point of view nothing has changed, an "ongoing situation. There is info, and there is correct info. They are false statements from the ministry, and it's not the first time."

He didn't want to comment any further on the matter.

It is not surprising Watson, alias Sam Selezny is not very willing to talk. He and his firm came under fire only recently during a broadcast from the VPRO. This broadcast even lead to questions being asked in Parliament (about the license).

The radio producers had contacted the sheriff of Santa Cruz, who confirmed the arrest of Watson on March the 20th in 1985, in relation to illegal cannabis growing.

How it was possible Watson could set foot in Holland a month later [4-20], no one understands. Why wasn't he, caught red-handed, in prison? As a rule the American Justice system doesn't show clemency to drug criminals.

There are presumptions, also mentioned in the radio program. Is it possible Watson struck a deal with American government, mainly the DEA? In other words, has he, in exchange for his freedom agreed to cooperate with the justice system from time to time?

Questions which are left unanswered.

The DEA never talks, something the survey committee "van Tra" discovered too.

On the 5th of November, Minister [Els] Borst answered the questions in Parliament.

No, there had not been a prior investigation in regards to the person requesting the license.

There had been doubts though about the reliability of the request, especially whether the cannabis would only be used for scientific purposes. But there was no proof to turn these doubts into hard facts. On the basis of doubt a license could not be rejected, in the court of law.

Actively requesting personal information from the police register had never been done, but she was planning to do so in due course.

Subject closed.

But the case is even stranger than it actually seems.

How did Watson acquire the funds to found HortaPharm? After some research it shows Watson wasn't only involved in illegal weed growing in the USA, but in Holland too. Not weedgrowing as a hobby, but on a grand scale, a business worth millions.

It was clear the Dutch Wietgrowers caught a big fish with getting David Watson on board. A man fascinated by the secrets of the cannabis plant. A man on a mission, convinced of the blessings of cannabis.

Like every American, he thought big. Just like Michael Taylor, also known as Michael Rich. They became companions, throwing themselves on the big scale growing of nederwiet.

Wernard Bruining declined. "It became too big and too fanatic. They wanted to be the best and biggest, which wasn't necessary for me."

It was annoying for him though that two of his greenhouses were busted shortly afterwards. A coincidence, the police told him, they just happened to come across it. "But it was the first time they busted a big greenhouse. Before that they had never managed to do so."

In the summer two big sites where busted, the third empty upon arrival. Various employees where arrested, Watson and Taylor stayed out of sight. In the "us knows us" world of growing they were already for some time known as people who pulled the strings. Shortly afterwards stories circulated the two Americans had started again. Within a few months they had set up a new greenhouse. This one was busted too, but again no sign of the Americans.

Were they simply too smart, or was it something else, something invisible (untouchable)?

No one paid too much attention to it. There were suspicions, but they were erased when the two continued a few years later, undisturbed.

It was the era when partially thanks to Watson's seed, Holland's masses switched to nederwiet.

It became an internationally recognized product, the new pearl of the Dutch horticulture.

But in 1992 the calm tide turned, when in the vicinity of Tilburg, two massive growsites were busted with, according to the police, 40,000 plants.

Sirens, SWAT teams, broken doors and a lot of screaming. Two of the approximately fifteen suspects broke down practically straight away under questioning and mentioned the name Watson as the big man and investor behind the wiet operation. Justice didn't act. Didn't ask questions about him, didn't even investigate the large amount of funds which apparently left the country via Luxembourg.

Watson was and remained, to the surprise of many, a free man and founded HortaPharm that same year.

Supported by advisers, he started negotiating with the health ministry about acquiring a license. One of these advisors was ex-police commissioner K. Sietsema, at that time already active as a private detective. "If I know HortaPharm? If we're talking about the same firm then yes, " Sietsema says; "but I don't talk about my clients, a kind of code of honor"

In the world of the wiet growers suspicion arose. One after the other growsite was busted, tens of people disappeared behind bars, but one of the biggest, and probably best could continue without any disturbances?

That the American Godfather of Nederwiet had such good contacts that he could continue to practice his profession legally for three years, the ultimate breeders' dream, was considered utterly strange.

Coincidence?

The arrest in 1985, the large-scale busts of grow sites without any consequences for Watson or his companion, HortaPharm and its first license, the advisor Sietsema, it was too much of a good thing.

Were Watson and Rich DEA informers after all, as some people had before claimed them to be?

"They started on the right side, but Watson had little choice," Bruining thinks. "It was either going to jail or cooperate with the American justice system."

Mario Lap, who amongst other things advises the PVDA (Dutch political party) on drugs problems, is sure of his case.

His last bit of doubt disappeared upon discovering that the Australian Police were in possession of a list, compiled by Watson, of renowned Dutch breeders, including a precise description of their products, even mentioning the genetic codes. Handy, with the eye on the plans of the Ministry of Health to make growing indoors illegal.

"Instantly those creeps have the monopoly, later on they'll be the only ones allowed to breed the seeds, which is what it is about," Lap says bitterly.

Which would make the DEA mission successful. They have the names of the breeders, their products and eventually the market of nederweed in hands.

The DEA has thus proven not only to be champion of controlled drug flow, but has also proven itself to be the best wiet grower in the world.

Copyright: *HP/De Tijd* 5-12-1997.

PvdA-fractie

1

*Op pag. 2[1] staat dat op 22 augustus 1991 «Research Seeds D. Watson»
een aanvraag heeft ingediend. Hoe verhoudt deze mededeling zich tot het
gestelde in de antwoorden op Kamervragen d.d. 13 oktober 1997 nr.
243, Aanhangsel Handelingen TK, vergaderjaar 1997–1998 dat Hortapharm in
1994 een aanvraag heeft ingediend? Betreft het hier verschillende
aanvragen? Zo ja, wat is het verschil tussen deze aanvragen?*

Aanvankelijk heeft Research Seeds D. Watson een aanvraag voor een
opiumverlof gedaan op 22 augustus 1991. Dit bedrijf is later voortgezet
onder de naam Hortapharm B.V. Het opiumverlof is uiteindelijk verleend
op 16 september 1994 (en dus niet aangevraagd in 1994, zoals de
antwoorden op bovengenoemde Kamervragen naar nu blijkt abusievelijk
vermelden). Het betreft geen verschillende aanvragen.

2

*In de beantwoording van de Kamervragen van 13 oktober 1997 wordt
vermeld dat Hortapharm destijds stelde dat de daadwerkelijke productie
in het buitenland zou plaatsvinden. Heeft deze ook daadwerkelijk
plaatsgevonden? In het artikel in HP/de Tijd van 5 december wordt
vermeld dat men op de hoogte is van het greenhouse van Hortapharm. Is
dit bericht juist?*

In welke mate productie buiten de landsgrenzen door Hortapharm
plaatsvindt valt buiten de waarnemingssfeer van de Nederlandse
overheid. Op deze vraag kan dan ook geen absoluut antwoord worden
gegeven. Wel is bekend dat de heer Watson in het Verenigd Koninkrijk een
bedrijf heeft opgericht voor de productie van medicinale hennep.
Het artikel in HP/de Tijd stelt dat de journalist bekend is met de plaats van
het greenhouse van Hortapharm. Ik kan dat bevestigen noch ontkennen.

3

*Is het waar dat Hortapharm beschikte over exportvergunningen
afgegeven door de Amerikaanse Drugs Enforcement Administration
(DEA)?
Hoe betrouwbaar is de mededeling daarover in het reeds aangehaalde
artikel van HP/de Tijd van 5 december 1997?*

Vermoedelijk berust het op een vergissing dat Hortapharm over een
exportvergunning van de DEA zou hebben beschikt. De DEA geeft im- en
exportvergunningen af aan Amerikaanse vergunninghouders voor de in-
en uitvoer vanuit de Verenigde Staten.
Mij is bekend dat de DEA aan een hoogleraar biologie van de Universiteit
van Indiana een importvergunning heeft verleend voor 100 gram
cannabiszaad, te betrekken van Hortapharm.
Hortapharm zelf is een in Nederland werkzame onderneming die zich voor
imen exportvergunningen moet wenden tot de Nederlandse overheid, in
casu de Inspectie voor de Gezondheidszorg (IGZ). In dat opzicht is de IGZ
de pendant van de DEA.
In de Verenigde Staten is een in- of uitvoervergunning van de DEA vereist
voor de in- of uitvoer van hennepzaad op grond van de Controlled
Substances Import and Export Act. In Nederland is dat niet het geval,
omdat hennepzaad niet onder de Opiumwet valt.

4

*Wat is de rol van de Amerikaanse DEA in de zaak Hortapharm? Welke
waarde dient men toe de kennen aan de mededelingen daarover in
eerdergenoemd artikel in HP/de Tijd?*

[1] Van de brief van de Minister van VWS aan
de Voorzitter van de Vaste Commissie voor
Volksgezondheid, Welzijn en Sport, d.d. 16
april 1999, kenmerk GMV 993 112, inzake de
stand van zaken Hortapharm.

Dutch government discussion of HortaPharm

CHAPTER 9

HortaPharm

You see, they don't want you using your drugs.
They want you to use their drugs.

– Chris Rock

Accorsding to Wikipedia: "The business was founded by David Paul Watson in 1990. He was soon joined by David W. Pate and eventually Robert C. Clarke. They obtained the first license issued by the Dutch government to permit a Cannabis research facility in the Netherlands. HortaPharm B.V. has a partnership with GW Pharmaceuticals to develop Cannabis varieties for the manufacture of pharmaceuticals.

"Using selective breeding and production control, HortaPharm created Cannabis strains that produce virtually single cannabinoids, approximately 98% THC or cannabidiol, relative to the total of other cannabinoids present."

Research Seeds D. Watson, a sole proprietorship, submitted an application for a drugs "leave" for scientific purposes on August 22, 1991. The name was later changed to HortaPharm B.V. The company was awarded the leave to operate outside national legal statues, specifically the Opium Act, and grow cannabis for research. The leave was granted on September 16, 1994, and ended September 16, 1997. HortaPharm submitted various other leaves, but these were all rejected.

There had been many problems, the first government inspection on June 30, 1995 deemed that accurate records were not being kept, and there was a request in writing for HortaPharm to clean up their act. A second inspection took place September 20, 1996; again accurate records were not being kept, and the amount of marijuana was way above the limit of the leave. Plus HortaPharm was using resources and equipment well beyond what the leave permitted.

Letters were again sent to HortaPharm. Finally on May 1, 1997, a letter was sent from Netherlands' Healthcare Inspectorate that re-stated the leave, strongly demanded that precise records be kept, and warned HortaPharm that if they could not straighten up within eight weeks, the leave would be withdrawn. On June 20, 1997 Hor-taPharm wrote and said they would be good.

A "third-party" inspection took place on August 7, 1997, and the findings were the same as earlier ones. On September 16, 1997 the leave expired, the reason: "detection of irregularities."

In early 1998 it came to the attention of the Inspectorate that HortaPharm was simply continuing their work as if they had the drug leave, and on April 8 the Inspectorate asked "Prosecution" to conduct an investigation, and, if necessary, to act.

The Inspectorate later received information from the Public Prosecutor that for reasons "not yet made public at this time" some-thing prevents them from bringing a case against HortaPharm.

Because of the "HortaPharm experience," the Inspectorate be-gan work on a modification of the Opium Act, which, among other things would allow the Inspectorate to refuse a leave if there is a "risk that the leave will be used to commit criminal offenses."

On May 26, 1998 HortaPharm submitted a new application for "chemical analytical purposes, breeding and submitted conservation of plant varieties, and import and export." Following up on the appli-cation there was an inspection on April 13, 1999. The inspector found large quantities of marijuana, and "enriched plant material consisting of resin parts with an estimated THC content of over 30%. In addition, the inspector determined that HortaPharm [was] not functioning at a level of quality thinking. There is no quality manual and there are no standardized procedures." The application was denied on April 14th.

From the parliamentary hearing in August of 1999: "Is it true that HortaPharm has export licenses issued by the DEA?" Yes, there was knowledge of at least one, where the DEA had granted 100 grams of cannabis seeds for a professor at the University of In-diana that involved HortaPharm.

Questions were asked in Parliament about the fact that if HortaPharm's leave was expired in Sept of 1997, and the fact that the April 1999 inspection found a large quantity of cannabis: "Does this mean that the company has committed crimes? If so, what Legal steps are then taken?"

"The conclusion seems justified that there are ... criminal offenses."

But for reasons that *"cannot yet be made public,"* no charges will be filed.

An exchange with a government Minister in a 1999 Lower House session:

> "Is it still true that the Prosecution under non-public information currently cannot act?
> "Yes.
> "Is the Minister aware of the grounds that prevent this to occur?
> "Yes, at least in broad outline.
> "This all means that HortaPharm is still continuing his work as if he still has his leave?
> "Yes."

Let me repeat what Watson had to say in late 1997 about the Minister's ability to close his doors. From the article "Thanks to Uncle Sam":

> "There are people who want it that way," he said was his cryptic explanation, "but there are also people who want it in a different way."

Here are a few newspaper articles about HortaPharm, notice that only the Dutch paper relates any of HortaPharm's difficulties.

HortaPharm Article in Dutch Newspaper
Trouw is a Dutch daily newspaper.

> *Trouw,* July 18, 1998
> (Translated)
>
> Controversial Medi-weed firm HortaPharm has again requested a license from the ministry of Health. The request follows after

recently Minister Borst informed the firm they are not allowed to trade in THC. HortaPharm has made an appeal in court against that decision. The ministry has had issues with the firm for a few years now. In September 1994 HortaPharm was granted a license. The license meant they were allowed to grow cannabis for research purposes in greenhouses in Aalsmeer.

This research entailed breeding weed with the aim to get the THC content as high as possible. According to the firm, pure THC can benefit appetite in Aids patients, and lessens sickness of cancer patients undergoing chemo, and helps MS patients.

A synthetic version of THC, Marinol, has already been on the market for years in North America, Israel, Australia, South Africa and Puerto Rico.

According to David Watson, owner of HortaPharm, the cannabis derived product is significantly cheaper and in the long run better than Marinol, which would make it a serious competitor for the pharmaceutical industry. He doesn't understand why the Dutch Government does not allow him to have access to this lucrative market. A market which he estimates to be a least a hundred million guilders.

Documents from the ministry of health show HortaPharm has linked itself with British firm Generics in Potters Bar. A twenty year agreement had been signed to develop the medicine "Naturbinol" on the basis of HortaPharm's seed produced in Holland.

HortaPharm also has linked itself with Institut für Onkologische und Immunologische Forschung in Berlin. Both Generics and the Berlin Institute claim HortaPharm's seeds are beneficial to them. But HortaPharm is not allowed to trade these seeds. Cannabis seed trading is allowed, but not the trading of THC. HortaPharm was provided with a one-time-only export license, for non-commercial research purposes. Watson continues to fight for a trade license in Holland, and has said the commercial part of his firm has been moved to the UK, under GW. Only the delivery of technology and seeds continues from Holland.

From a unpublished statement of the commission of complaints of the ministry of health, however, some remarkable facts arise. These facts don't only say something about HortaPharm itself, but about the people involved in the inspection too.

Then in September a license was granted on the basis that HortaPharm would act "good and trustworthy" under the license. The minister states however that the firm, despite several warnings, didn't keep to the agreement. HortaPharm grew a significantly larger amount than necessary for THC extraction. During an inspection, 250 kilos of Cannabis, 12 kilos of shredded cannabis and cannabis oil were found. The administration of the firm had not been done according to regulation and plants were not destroyed in the prescribed way. The latter meant a notary act of the destruction needed to have been written.

The 250 kilos of cannabis would provide 25 kilos of THC, while the amount of THC HortaPharm was allowed to have on premises was 10 grams. Watson denies fervently that the firm has messed with the paperwork. Apparently part of the paperwork was sent to the minister but had gotten lost there.

Whether Watson has done dodgey things with his firm has not really been investigated. It is remarkable however that, despite the ministerial warnings, the firm was simply allowed to continue for three years. It is even more remarkable considering the fact that during question time in Parliament last year, minister Borst already claimed there were doubts whether HortaPharm only grew hemp for science purposes.

Despite all these doubts HortaPharm is still trading and Watson continues his battle for a license in Holland. Factually speaking, the firm trades on a license which has run out. In legal terms that means HortaPharm is an illegal weed growing business.

The general ministry is aware of the situation, but doesn't wish to comment about the matter for the foreseeable future.

Copyright trouw.nl

A week after the above news article appeared, HortaPharm was mentioned in a press release in the United Kingdom.

GW Pharmaceuticals Press Release

Details released of collaboration between GW Pharmaceuticals and HortaPharm medicinal cannabis 23 July 1998

Details have been disclosed of the collaboration between GW Pharmaceuticals – the British Company licensed by the Home

Office to conduct research into the medicinal uses of cannabis –
and Dutch medicinal cannabis plant breeding company Horta-
Pharm B.V. Speaking at the International Cannabinoid Research
Society (ICRS) conference in Montpellier, Dr. Geoffrey W.
Guy, Chairman of GW Pharmaceuticals, said that HortaPharm
will provide GW with exclusive access to its entire range of cannabis varieties for the development of medicines.

The worldwide rights acquired by GW for an undisclosed
sum cover varieties grown to date with certain exceptions and
all varieties to be bred in future. Plant registrations arising from
the Dutch breeding programme will be owned by GW. Under
the agreement GW will be responsible for the development of
specific drug delivery technologies to administer the pharmaceutical grade medicinal cannabis.

This work will include a vaporizer for which HortaPharm has
a patent pending. In addition GW will fund HortaPharm's botanical research and HortaPharm scientists will assist in the UK
Glasshouse propagation, cloning and cultivation programme.

Dr. Guy, said: "There has been much speculation as to the
exact role of the various chemical components of cannabis in
treating patients with illnesses such as Multiple Sclerosis and
AIDS wasting syndrome. In particular THC (the psychoactive
constituent chemical) has received much attention. Historical
medical reports and more recent work may point to the influence of cannabidiol (CBD) in epilepsy and stroke for example.
We wish to explore the therapeutic benefits and the potential
for reduction in unwanted effects that may be offered through
administration of complete extracts containing various defined
ratios of the principal cannabinoids."

Mr David Watson, Chief Executive of HortaPharm com-
mented: "HortaPharm leads the world in its understanding
of cannabis botany and has built up over many years the most
extensive 'Living Library' of Medicinal Cannabis varieties. As
soon as Dr. Guy's clinical research indicates the exact desired
composition our scientists can breed and register new medicinal varieties."

GWPharma – Details released of collaboration between GW
Pharmaceuti... http://www.gwpharm.com/23july1998.
© GW Pharmaceuticals.

British Newspaper article

Then in September of 1998, came a very interesting article from *The Independent*, a British national morning newspaper.

Cannabis: a year that changed minds

The medical benefits of the drug are now widely accepted. Vanessa Thorpe meets the research team developing a plant that could transform lives

The Independent

Vanessa Thorpe

Sunday, 27 September 1998

NOT EVERY Dutch greenhouse the aeroplanes fly over on the descent to the runway at Schipol airport is full of tulip bulbs. One cluster of glass outhouses, in particular, contains a very different crop.

At a secret location between the airport and the city of Amsterdam, a small team of highly motivated scientists is working on the world's first patented cannabis plant product. So far, their chief and only customer is a British doctor.

Slide back the door to one of HortaPharm's large greenhouses and the smell is overwhelming. Rows of cannabis plants of different types and sizes stretch out into the middle distance. But, contrary to appearances, this research farm is no paradise for the pleasure-seeking puffer.

"It looks like dope, but really it's hope," explains the proprietor, American entrepreneur David Watson. What he means is that many of these plants have been specifically bred not to produce an intoxicating resin or hashish. Indeed, HortaPharm hopes to thwart the aims of the average recreational user.

The team are already close to finding their own commercial Holy Grail – seeds that will produce a one-off, female, seedless crop of plants with no psychotropic effects (or THC highs, to the layman) for the consumer. Why, you might ask, would they want to do that?

The answer is that Mr Watson and his Amsterdam-based scientists are working to create a stable, plant-based medical product. They want to isolate the beneficial effects of cannabis' various properties and then reproduce them, ad infinitum, from specialized parent plants.

Mr Watson and his Dutch colleague, biochemist Etienne de Meijer, are confident that by using their own exclusive cross-breeding methods, they can develop healthy plants which will combine only the desired chemical make-up of individual medicines.

There will be no generational deterioration and no genetic difference between each plant because they will be bred from themselves: they will be cloned. "You can clone a plant 10 times," explains Mr de Meijer, "and every time it will be exactly the same."

Mr de Meijer has developed his own technique of "self-progeny" – or "selfing" – where he turns half of one female plant temporarily into a male. Fertilizing a plant with itself in this way means the same genetic make-up can be reproduced.

"I can make 20,000 clones with 'selfed' parents in two weeks," he says. "Humans may degenerate from inbreeding, but these plants do not. I'm sure I am the first person to apply this method of inbreeding to cannabis and I found the selfing process was amazingly simple."

But the unique research has no market in Holland. "Because the sale of the drug is tolerated in coffee shops, there is no interest – though people don't really know what they are buying," says Mr Watson.

As a result, the seeds that HortaPharm is producing are passed straight on to Britain to take their place in the soil at the ground-breaking facility set up this summer by Dr. Geoffrey Guy in south-east England. "We hooked up with Dr. Guy in January and right now all we are doing is providing the basic building blocks for his work," says Mr Watson. "We were rather surprised that it would happen in England first."

HortaPharm's sample plants are analyzed in the laboratory with a gas chromatographer and with each new batch the team homes in on the plant's distinct chemical components or cannabinoids – THC, CBD, CBC, CBG and THCV. When Dr. Guy completes his medical research in Britain, HortaPharm will breed plants to supply the right combination of active ingredients for his treatments. "Once Dr. Guy has worked out what he wants in chemical form, we will find him the right physical characteristics, too, by combining desirable features from plants found around the world – high-resin production and resistance to disease," says Mr de Meijer.

HortaPharm is only interested in developing female plants that are sterile, but this is not just to protect their genetic copyright. "If a plant is not kept busy producing seeds, all its energy can go into resin production," says Mr de Miejer.

Sitting at his computer screen in Amsterdam, Mr Watson can keep an eye on the perimeter fence at Dr. Guy's British farm via the Internet. "The security he has there is amazing," says Mr Watson, who flew out to plant the first seeds there two months ago.

In June, Dr. Guy's company, GW Pharmaceuticals, secured the first British license to grow the plant for medical purposes. By arrangement with the Home Office, the doctor can farm cannabis plants and investigate their properties with a view to marketing a cheap herbal-based answer to the debilitating symptoms of MS, Glaucoma, Parkinson's, cancer, asthma and Aids.

A year ago today the Independent on Sunday launched its campaign to decriminalize cannabis, attracting tremendous public attention. Five months later, the IoS held a march, attended by more than 16,000 people, and organised an influential Westminster Conference to look at drugs legislation. Yesterday, hundreds of campaigners met again in Hyde Park to demonstrate their continuing concerns.

But it is the case for legalizing the medical use of the drug which has gained most ground in the past 12 months. Key markers of this shift in public perspective were the positive outcome of the British Medical Association's report in November last year and the House of Lords' select committee decision to investigate the question. The committee has yet to publish its conclusions.

This week, even more powerful evidence of the useful properties of cannabis was revealed in the work of the research team working under Dr. Ian Meng at the University of California. Researching on rats, Dr. Meng has found the brain stem circuit which is involved in the pain-suppressing activities of morphine, but which is also activated by the consumption of cannabinoids. "The medical arguments are really gaining ground," says Dr. Meng. "There is some proof now that the drug can help people."

Dr. Guy also believes scientifically verifiable research is the only way forward. Although he is looking at anecdotal patient evidence, he knows that outside the laboratory it is impossible to establish exactly which cannabinoids are effective.

Mr Watson of HortaPharm makes the same point: "Domestic users can make a contribution, but they don't know the profile of the plant they are treating themselves with. The average hashish in a coffee-shop product is 5 per cent THC. We can already make it 30 per cent. So, what are they doing to it?" He believes the bright future of the drug is contained in the greenhouses of HortaPharm and GW Pharmaceuticals.

At his Amsterdam glasshouses, he nods conspiratorially at the healthy-looking garden produce. "Don't say anything yet, but we are also working on putting THC into tomatoes," he confides. Then he cackles reassuringly: "Only kidding!"

© independent.co.uk

And on it goes ...

From the *Journal of Forensic Sciences*:

Datwyler, S. L. and Weiblen, G. D. (2006), Genetic Variation in Hemp and Marijuana (Cannabis sativa L.) According to Amplified Fragment Length Polymorphisms.

*HortaPharm B.V. (the Netherlands) and Kenex Ltd. (Canada) provided controlled substances for research registered and permitted by the United States Drug Enforcement Administration and the Minnesota Board of Pharmacy with support from the David and Lucille Packard Foundation and the Minnesota Agricultural Experiment Station. The study was first presented at the Botanical Society of America Annual Meeting in 2004 at Snowbird, Utah.

From the *TokeSignals*:

Worth Repeating:
It's Official! Cannabinoids Kill All Types of Cancer

By Ron Marczyk On March 15, 2013.

The US Patent & Trade Office on March 7, 2013 granted GW Pharma a medical patent covering all plant-based phytocannabinoids for use in the treatment and prevention of basically all forms of human cancer.

Entitled: PHYTOCANNABINOIDS IN THE TREATMENT OF CANCER
United States Patent Application # 20130059018
Assignee: GW Pharma
Publication Date: 03/07/2013
Filing Date: 03/11/2011

> http://www.freepatentsonline.com/y2013/0059018.html

All phytocannabinoids? As in the plural? As in covering every chemical this plant makes and its use in the treatment of human cancer?

The back story: On 1/17/2013, the National Cancer Institute updated its Cannabis and Cannabinoids PDQ® webpage with the following new cannabis and cancer information, which just by coincidence supports the new GW Pharma pre-approved patent and lays the groundwork for GW Pharma's future new breakout marijuana-based cancer drugs.

> http://www.cancer.gov/cancertopics/pdq/cam/cannabis/
> healthprofessional/page4

From Cannabis and Cannabinoids (PDQ®) Last Modified: 01/17/2013

Cannabinoids may cause anti-tumor effects by various mechanisms, including induction of cell death, inhibition of cell growth, and inhibition of tumor angiogenesis invasion and metastasis.

One review summarizes the molecular mechanisms of action of cannabinoids as anti-tumor agents. Cannabinoids appear to kill tumor cells but do not affect their non-transformed counterparts and may even protect them from cell death.

These compounds have been shown to induce apoptosis in glioma cells (a type of brain cancer) in culture and induce regression of glioma tumors in mice and rats. Cannabinoids protect normal glial cells of astroglial and oligodendroglial lineages from apoptosis mediated by the CB1 receptor.

> http://www.cancer.gov/cancertopics/pdq/cam/cannabis/
> healthprofessional/page4

Read: Cannabinoids from plant sources cause immortalized cancer cells to die, stops them from growing and shuts down their needed blood supply, all while not harming healthy cells, unlike chemotherapy and radiation.

More back story information:

Below is the same type of National Cancer Institute Cannabis and Cannabinoids PDQ® update that appeared on March 17, 2011 but was censored and removed in only 11 days: that was two years ago.

> The potential effects of medicinal cannabis for people living with cancer include antiemetic effects, appetite stimulation, pain relief, and improved sleep. In the practice of integrative oncology the health care provider may recommend medicinal cannabis not only for symptom management but also for its possible direct anti-tumor effect.

Presently:

The new government-supported information promoted this strong reaction by The Advocates for the Disabled and Seriously Ill in the story below.

March 12, 2013:

Federal Government Reports Marijuana Effective in Combating Certain Cancers, Reports ADSI

The NCI report examined whether patients who smoke marijuana rather than ingesting it orally are exposed to a higher risk of lung and certain digestive system cancers..."

NCI, according to the government, 19 studies "failed to demonstrate statistically significant associations between marijuana inhalation and lung cancer." The report also identified a separate study of 611 lung cancer patients that showed marijuana was "not associated with an increased risk of lung cancer or other upper aero digestive tract cancers and found no positive associations with any cancer type."

In its report, the National Cancer Institute also identified a "study of intratumoral injection of delta-9-THC in patients with recurrent glioblastoma [brain cancer] that showed tumor reduction in the test participants."

In addition to anti-cancer properties, separate research reported marijuana appears to have "profound nerve-protective and brain-enhancing properties that could potentially treat many neurodegenerative disorders."

Dr. Donald Tashkin, UCLA:

"It turned out that increased marijuana use did not result in higher rates of lung and pharyngeal cancer, whereas tobacco smokers were at greater risk the more they smoked. Tobacco smokers who also smoked marijuana were at slightly lower risk of getting lung cancer than tobacco-only smokers."

PHYTOCANNABINOIDS IN THE TREATMENT OF CANCER /March 7, 2013

United States Patent Application # 20130059018
Assignee: GW Pharma

This invention relates to the use of phytocannabinoids, either in an isolated form or in the form of a botanical drug substance [isn't that cannabis?] In the treatment of cancer. Preferably the cancer to be treated is cancer of the prostate, cancer of the breast or cancer of the colon.

Researchers however have discovered that some cannabinoids, including THC and cannabidiol (CBD) are able to promote the re-emergence of apoptosis (the signal for a cell to die) so that some tumors will heed the signals, stop dividing, and die.

Another method by which tumors grow is by ensuring that they are nourished: they send out signals to promote angiogenesis, the growth of new blood vessels. Cannabinoids may turn off these signals as well.

In summary these data demonstrate the protective effects of phytocannabinoids in the PREVENTION of colon cancer. Of significance is the phytocannabinoids CBG which exerts a strong protective effect against colon cancer particularly when it is in an isolated form.

Pay no attention to the fact that cannabis use predates human civilization. How do you make it illegal for people but not corporations? People deserve qual treatment under the law and access to medicine.

Patenting cannabis is like patenting corn and all the products it makes, and then telling me I can't grow corn in my backyard. How do you patent nature, restrict people's access to it and then charge them to use it while you are making a big profit?

The bad news in all of this?

This patent was pre-approved and was written to only include cannabis products made by GW Pharma.

GW's grow house operations. They don't sell marijuana, they sell medicine. See the difference?

Despite the Federal government sanctioned and authorized NCI report, Pappas said Congress and the Obama Administration have continued to thwart marijuana research. In an announced effort to displace state medical marijuana laws, the Office of National Drug Control Policy described 'medical' marijuana as a 'myth' fueling 'troubling misconceptions' in documents found on its website.

The Federal government appears to be focused on creating more chemical drugs, many of which are the subject of various attorney television commercials seeking out those adversely impacted by those drugs.

They will be fracking apart the plant and selling it back to you piecemeal in different cannabinoid ratios that they now own the rights to.

They will be trying to sell high-priced water at the river's edge.

Here comes the big payday that you're not going to be part of. How much will one month of Sativex wind up costing? My lowball guess is north of $2000/month X 12 =$24,000 per patient vs. The average monthly cost of cannabis use per patient at about $200-400 per month?

I propose the U.S. government nationalize this new fledgling marijuana industry as a cooperative nationwide network of American people, and not of corporations.

This reasoning is based on two counts:

We, the people of the U.S., own the first patent on this plant since back in 2003.

This should be reparation to the people, to try to heal the 75-year war we have waged on ourselves out of ignorance.

How about we, the American people, win for once?

GW Pharma is really part of a conglomeration of international pharmaceutical corporations that just patented a plant you can grow in your backyard and will control its use in cancer treatment. I'm sure they have our best interests at heart.

Copyright: Ron Marczyk

CHAPTER 10

Sam Sez

In 2006, I joined International Cannagraphic's online forums. Someone had started a thread about Reinhard Delp's Ice Water Method titled, "The 'inventor' lawsuits for ice hash kits." This was started by "Aroma" on March 20, 2006. Which was ironically the same date, twenty-one years earlier, when David Watson was reportedly busted in the Santa Cruz, California area, and then showed up in Amsterdam one month later as Sam "Skunkman" Selezny.

As I noted earlier, I had met Delp in 2005, and soon started using and promoting his X-Tractor 1000. He told me the troubles that he was having, and of the attempts to confuse his patent rights. He shared with me his documents and correspondence. I began to get upset about what was being done.

Delp had started in 1998 to actively try and protect the patent he had filed in 1997. There was an article in *Hanf*, a German marijuana magazine about the origins of the method being used in the XTR 1000. Delp's Swiss company requested and received a retraction:

> In regards to *Hanf* Issue February 1998 – "Ancient Methods in ModernTimes"
>
> Due to patent right issues, Swiss Ice Cold GmbH demands this retraction.
>
> "The Ice Water Method" was invented in California, by one of our partners, and the Pollinator Company/Amsterdam distributes our products in the European Union.

Delp continued to work with Mila Jansen. He asked her to honor her agreement, and confronted her at the '98 Cannabis Cup while she was demonstrating the Ice-O-Lator. Her comment to Delp: "Have you read Bob's book [*Hashish!*]?"

Then came a July 1999 article in *Hanf*, "Water Made Hash – the Water Extraction Method with the Ice-O-Later," which talked about Jansen, Clarke's book, *Hashish!*, and Sadu Sam's Secret, "a water extraction technique (invented by Nevil from the Cannabis Castle) ... He [Clarke] also cites Sadu Sam's original instructions, which suggest the use of an outboard motor in a 55 Gallon drum.... The Swiss Ice Cold-machine [X-Tractor 1000], which was introduced at the Cannabis Cup, is in principle nothing else but a 20 Liter bucket with a mixer on the top and a screen on the bottom." The article then went on to speak of Jansen and her Ice-O-Later.

Delp through his Swiss company wrote an email response to *Hanf* in early September 1999, along with several attached exhibits that laid out his case. Later that month he sent a letter and copies of documents to Red Eye Press. He wrote:

> For your information we send you a translation of our response to a 7/98 article in "Hanf" a German magazine which relates to your publication: HASHISH! Robert Connell Clarke, 98. Your author's very unprofessional if not fraudulent behavior in not relating "his findings" to our Xtractor introduction in 97 and instead promoting "his own Xtractor" and now Mila Jansen's I-O-Later; is causing us considerable damage!

I have referenced earlier the reply Delp received, where Red Eye Press publisher, James Goodwin, praised his nom-de-plume's editing capabilities. From Red Eye Press' November 1999 reply:

> You state that Sadu Sam's advice to "grind" the material is the wrong approach. I would think that you would take this evidence that Sadu Sam's method predated yours, since your method improved the procedure. All hashish-makers thank you.... I have just looked at one of the many disks that Mel Frank [Goodwin] generated while editing *Hashish!* The disk has the computer generated date of a Sadu Sam file of June 1996.... Ideas are neither copyright nor patent protected. Sadu Sam understands this, otherwise he might be after you for stealing *his* idea. [Emphasis in original.]

Interestingly, Goodwin/Frank wrote that Delp's "method improved the procedure," but then moved the discussion to the legal arena, asking Delp to send any new correspondence lawyer to lawyer

Hanf used Goodwin's letter to deflect Delp's request for retraction or any explanation. Delp also wrote a letter to *High Times* in September 1999.

> The subject might be of interest to you.
>
> Herewith I send you, what I would call: "Chronicle of a rip-off." It is a translation of a response to a German "HANF" magazine article (7/99) in which the newest invention of the Pollinator Comp. ... their "I(ce)- 0- later," is introduced and Robert Ronnel [*sic*] Clarke's book "Hashish" claims origin. Unlike "HIGH TIMES" (see May 98) Clarke doesn't mention our surprise introduction of the "XTR 420" on your Cup 97 in his book. Instead he introduces his own "XTRACTOR" and his own cool water method....
>
> We thank HIGH TIMES for the excellent journalism and truly independent reporting.

What happened next? *High Times* ran an article in its April 2000 issue (release – January 2000) about making hash. The pictures were by "Mel Frank," the piece was co-written by Frank (Goodwin), with a credit to Clarke's *Hashish*! The article repeated the Sadu Sam genesis of water extraction by way of "Nevil 'King of the Cannabis Castle,'" but changed the instructions from cold water to now use "ice water." The article didn't mention the Ice-O-Later by name, but did mention Jansen's Pollinator: "To get the best yields when processing for commercial quantities, helpful implements can be adapted from everyday tools.... In this instance we did use the flexible nylon screens obtained from the Pollinator Company.... The nylon screens, also called cleaner bags ..."

Even though, just a few months earlier, Frank as Goodwin had written to Delp that his procedure had improved the method and wrote: "All hashish-makers thank you for your input." There was no mention of Delp, his machine or his improved method. The rip off moved along.

By the time I had met Delp in 2005, the charade had continued with Jansen's Ice-O-Later, Bubbleman's bags and many other products using Delp's patented method. Delp had received his U.S. patent in 2000, and later his European and Canadian patents in 2006. Delp spent thousands of dollars defending his patents. He has been able to prevail in Germany, and only licensed products are available there. He has gone to court in Canada, getting a judgment against one firm, while other cases are still in the courts. He has had a hard time finding adequate representation in the Netherlands.

I told Delp I would help. I was incensed by the way he and his discovery were being treated, and jumped into the fray. I had been doing some writing, and a piece I had done about Nepal had run at Alexander Cockburn's CountterPunch.org in May 2005.

With Delp's documents, some Internet research, and my forty years experience in the hashish business, I wrote a new chapter for a new edition of my book, *King of Nepal*. I called it the Ice Wars Edition. An English writer, Annie Riecken had coined that term in 2001 for the brouhaha while doing research for the *Red Eye Express*, a small UK indie magazine reporting on the world cannabis scene.

I posted a short article, "Ice Wars: Or Who Invented The Bomb" that appeared on several websites, and did some interviews. This led to the posting in 2006 by Aroma at the International Cannagraphic's online forum.

Here is that post:

> The 'inventor' lawsuits for ice hash kits
> Read an article in CCnews 23. http://www.ccnewz.com (a free UK growing paper) about some prick called Joseph R Pietri "the inventor" who has patented some ice extraction device and to quote a little of the article :
>
>> "The inventor is currently seeking to enforce his original US patents on the ice water extraction process mentioned above. Lawsuits are likely to follow, in Europe as well as US and Canada, involving several well known names."
>
> I for one will not be ordering any of this sad individual's products. But include his website for your information. I highly suspect his threats are BS. What a complete and utter asshole.
> http://www.icecold.org/company.htm

After learning about the thread in the summer of 2006, I joined as "Will," (the forum only allowed aliases), and posted my two cents. Granted, I might have taken a different tack, but my better half had recently passed away, leaving me without her soft reflective grace. Add to that my natural Brooklyn tendencies, plus the outrage I felt at how Delp and others were being treated. And I didn't care to be called names, so I may have been a bit, let's say brusque.

I made my first post August 13, 2006, ending with: "I'll be making hash at the Cup this year as Swiss Ice Cold returns after 9 years. No way any bubble hash can come close to ice hash made the correct way!!!!"

On August 17 at 6:07 A.M., "Sam_Skunkman" posted:

FYI, I was in Afghanistan pre 1972 also, and the Brotherhood, some who were friends of mine, may have been amongst the first to bring back Indica Afghani seeds to the USA. So did I. Where are the Brotherhood Afghani Indica varieties? I still have mine. And of course the Haze was not developed in Hawaii, it was developed in Santa Cruz, California in the early 1970's from Colombian and Mexican seeds, by R.L. I know because I was there, I lived next door.

In the 1980's I offered a $10 instruction sheet in *High Times* to extract resin from buds using just cold water and a jar. Quite a few years later the Ice-o-later and Reinhardt [Delp] showed up in Amsterdam claiming to have invented ice-water sifting. Mila and Bubbleman both came later. But Reinhardt's method is a slight change to my published water method, I said the colder the water the better, he said use ice water. But his method does not work without water, it is not the ice that makes it work it is the cold water in fact. Ice improves the yield.

I never said his patent would not be granted, I said the patent would not be enforceable because of my prior publishing of the water sifting method.

At 7:14 A.M. "Sam_Skunkman" posted:

I agree that Will or anyone else who is a rat and should be banned from ICMF for outing Soma's or anyone's real name. A rat is a rat is a rat is a rat. Some people think it is OK to rat out people they think are bad people, I DO NOT AGREE. Ratting out anyone is still ratting......

And I will have nothing to do with RATS!!!!

Does anyone agree?

-SamS

I posted at 8:28 A.M.:

Anyone I know who works for the police, well I pass the info on to everyone I know. Remember we are patented, we don't have to be quiet any longer. As you can see these guys are being investigated by the Culture. There is so much back-up evidence they have made a CDROM of the whole situation, over three hundred documented pieces of evidence of major fraud. My name is Joe Pietri [the name was obscured in the forum post] and I don't live in fear. I live in the light of truth.

At 8:38 A.M. "Sam_Skunkman" posted:

Will,

You are a snitch. You know what a snitch is? A RAT. I will be happy to see you in Amsterdam at the High Times Cannabis Cup and will be happy to give you a chance for you to "stick my foot up his ass." What a joke. I am laughing because it was me and Rob Clarke that gave Steve Hager at *High Times* the idea to have the first *High Times* Cannabis Cup. And by the way I won first place at the first *HT* Cannabis Cup.

This guy is dangerous, he is full of hate and lies. I advise everyone to stay far far away from him. He really thinks it is OK to RAT on people as long as he knows the person is bad according to him. God save us from fundamentalists who know they are right and know the ends justify the means, be they religious or just plain nuts.

-SamS

By 9:05 A.M. "Will" was banned from the forum.

Neither I, nor Delp have ever denied that Sadu Sam/Sam Skunkman/Sam Selezny/Dave Watson sold a water separation technique through *High Times*. Here is a copy of his ad from August 1987. Send $10 to Sadu Sam in Santa Cruz, California. Sadu Sam did his business in Santa Cruz while David Watson was in Amsterdam. Convenient.

Delp has copies of that paper you received for your ten dollars. There is no mention of ice or ice water, and the user is instructed: "The material is dried over a very low heat ... so that is crisp and dry.... The material is ground through a coarse screen or strainer. All dust and debris is collected ..." Delp's breakthrough came from ice and using undried material. Delp's process has less steps, and the end result is purer.

The Official Dealer McDope Game.

Though I was banned from posting, I did continue to read and gather some of the posts at International Cannagraphic. Let me share some "Sam Sez," some in response to the Ice War kerfuffle and, some from breeding-turf wars. Matter-of-fact, there appears to be quite a lot riding on who bred what, and who owns the different cannabis strains and their seeds. More on that later.

"Sam_Skunkman" public postings from International Cannagraphic's online forums (emphasis in original):

> THERE WERE NO FOUNDING MEMBERS OF SACRED SEEDS, JUST ME! ... Durbin Poison South Africa was developed by me alone, then I took it to Amsterdam. The same with Afghani #1, me alone.

> Skunk #1 was bred by me not some made up collective. I was not busted, did not go back and save clones. Never served a day. Never lost a single seed or plant in the USA.

> I mean Nevil [Schoenmaker] sold all my varieties to Sinsi Seeds when he closed the Seed Bank, for big $ and then told Ben

[Dronkers] they were never Nevil's to sell in the first place and I had spent years developing them ...

Both the Haze Bros were close friends of mine and both were close neighbors for years ...

Skunk #1 and Original Haze were famous for a decade or more before Nevil ever even thought of selling seeds, wise up. Nevil did ship to anyone across internetional[sic] borders, something I told him was stupid and would put him in jail. Who was right? When I met Nevil he had zero good seeds, he was selling imported Mex seeds and Colombian seeds and African seeds from coffee shop weed for $.25 cents each. They were crap. I gave him Skunk #1 and a few others and he repaid me a few years later by copying my varieties and selling them himself cutting me out, after promising he would not.

You were not there but RCC was there and can back me up ...

You say possession is 9/10s of the law so if I buy a pack of Shantibabas SSH [Super Silver Haze] I can then sell the SSH variety seeds to everyone? If that is what you mean then you are a low life dude, and I will put your posts on ignore or remove them from the thread.

Remember I am the Moderator for this thread.

G13 is not from University of Miss, I have been to the facility, I was invited to visit by Dr. ElSohly, I asked them about G13 and they looked in their records and said they never had a plant called G13, they did not even have clones until a few yeas ago.

Yes I introduced California Orange.

I was never in prison, this is just made up crap.

Not true at all, I never grew in a warehouse ever, and did not get busted ...

Well, at least that's what Sam sez ...

CHAPTER 11

Cannabis Cabal

David Watson aka Sam Skunkman/Sam Selezny and Robert C. Clarke are partners in HortaPharm, the only publicly-known private company that is licensed by DEA to produce and provide medicinal cannabis seeds of reliable quality for research.

A friend of mine, Bret Bogue, interviewed Danny Danko, a *High Times* cultivation editor, who had recently met with Watson. Bogue told Danko that Watson had said that he now had multiple DEA licenses, and that indeed he had supplied research and information to DEA. Danko walked away from this conversation with a pit in his stomach. Danko's book,

Danny Danko

The Official High Times Field Guide to Marijuana Strains was based on data supplied by Watson and Clarke. Information that obscures the true origins of medical strains, which are now being claimed by Watson, Clarke and others as intellectual property.

Begun in 1968, the only U.S. licensed cannabis-growing facility is at the University of Mississippi, where Dr. Carlton E. Turner worked from 1971-1981. Turner graduated from the University of Southern Mississippi, earning a bachelor's degree in chemistry and master's and doctoral degrees in organic chemistry. He became one of the nation's leading experts on the botany and pharmacology of marijuana.

Carlton Turner

Turner headed the Marijuana Research Project at the University of Mississippi. He served in the University's Research Institute for Pharmaceutical Studies, becoming Director of the Institute in 1980. He also worked as a consultant for government agencies and private firms in the United States, Mexico, and Canada, as well as for the United Nations.

Turner was appointed Senior Policy Adviser for Drug Policy in July 1981. In March 1982, his title changed to Director of the Drug Abuse Policy Office. He took on the additional title of Special Assistant to the President for Drug Abuse Policy in April 1983. In March 1985, he was appointed Deputy Assistant to the President for Drug Abuse Policy. Turner served as the President's adviser for drug abuse policy and assisted Nancy Reagan with her domestic and international drug abuse education projects. Turner left the White House staff effective December 31, 1986.

The university still produces the marijuana cigarettes for the four legal cannabis federal patients still being served today. The federal government's Compassionate Investigative New Drug program began in 1976 and stopped accepting new patients in 1992. The surviving patients still receive, monthly, a tin canister filled with about 300 pre-rolled marijuana cigarettes that have been essential to managing their conditions – a rare bone spur disorder, multiple sclerosis, glaucoma, and a painful condition called nail patella syndrome, respectively.

The federal government officially recognized cannabis' medical properties in 1985, when the FDA approved a prescription drug that is made of synthetic THC – Marinol – for nausea. But has kept marijuana as a Schedule I drug. The DEA definition: "Schedule I drugs, substances, or chemicals are defined as drugs with no currently accepted medical use and a high potential for abuse."

From Wikipedia: "The National Institute on Drug Abuse (NIDA) is a United States federal-government research institute whose mission is to lead the Nation in bringing the power of science to bear on drug abuse and addiction.… NIDA has a government granted monopoly on the production of medical marijuana for research purposes. In the past, the institute has refused to supply marijuana to researchers who had obtained all other necessary federal permits. Medical marijuana researchers and activists claim that NIDA, which is not supposed to be a regulatory organization, does not have the authority to effectively regulate who does and doesn't get to do research with medical marijuana.

"Jag Davies of the Multidisciplinary Association for Psychedelic Studies (MAPS) writes in MAPS Bulletin: 'Currently, the National Institute on Drug Abuse (NIDA) has a monopoly on the supply of research-grade marijuana, but no other Schedule I drug, that can be used in FDA-approved research. NIDA uses its monopoly power to obstruct research that conflicts with its vested interests. MAPS had two of its FDA-approved medical marijuana protocols rejected by NIDA, preventing the studies from taking place. MAPS has also been trying without success for almost four years to purchase 10 grams of marijuana from NIDA for research into the constituents of the vapor from marijuana vaporizers, a non-smoking drug delivery method that has already been used in one FDA-approved human study.'"

Times have been changing, though, as Wikipedia noted: "This article is outdated. Please update this section to reflect recent events or newly available information."

A March 18, 2014 article at leafscience.com, "U.S. Government Clears Way For Medical Marijuana Research in PTSD," notes:

> In a letter last Friday, the U.S. Department of Health and Human Services signed off on the team's proposal to trial medical marijuana as a treatment for PTSD.
>
> Researchers from Multidisciplinary Association for Psychedelic Studies (MAPS), led by Dr. Sue Sisley of the University of Arizona, can now move forward with the final step of purchasing marijuana from NIDA – the only legal source of marijuana for research purposes.
>
> "It really is a concrete advance in how the U.S. federal government is approaching medical marijuana drug development research," says Brad Burge, MAPS communications director.

"It clears the way for marijuana to actually be a prescription drug," he adds.

While medical marijuana has been legalized by various states, physicians can't go further than simply recommending it. Patients and doctors in legal states are also vulnerable to federal prosecution, notes Burge.

Since submitting their first request for research-grade cannabis in 1999, the team at MAPS faced numerous rejections. A previous proposal to study marijuana for PTSD was rejected by U.S. Health and Human Services in 2011.

But for some reason, Burge says, this time around was different.

The study is set to take place at the University of Arizona and will enroll 50 veterans with chronic, treatment-resistant PTSD. The researchers hope to demonstrate the effects of smoked and vaporized cannabis on symptoms of the disorder.

The group says its goal is to show that even smoked marijuana has medical value – as anecdotal evidence strongly suggests.

"The idea is to get marijuana – the whole plant – approved as a prescription drug that physicians can then prescribe," Burge explains. [Emphases not in original.]

What was different now? What had transpired during the last fifteen years? Crude marijuana was now legal in two states. Surely the old biases are going away. But as illustrated by excerpts from another article at leafscience.com on March 12, 2014, it is still a struggle to get cannabis research authorized:

The University of Colorado issued a memo Wednesday explaining to its faculty members why conducting research on marijuana is not nearly as easy as buying it.

Since changes were made to state law, a number of researchers at the university have expressed interest in carrying out studies on cannabis. School administrators responded on Wednesday by pointing out that federal law is still the same.

"It remains illegal under federal law for any person to import, manufacture, distribute, possess, or use marijuana," reads the memo written by University of Colorado President Bruce Benson and University Counsel Patrick O'Rourke.

Indeed, marijuana is not in fact legal in Colorado, as far as the federal government is concerned....

Last summer, the Justice Department gave Colorado and Washington the go-ahead to set up systems for regulating the sale of marijuana. Universities and research institutes, however, were not included in the deal.

"Institutions of higher education have an obligation to comply with federal drug laws as a condition of receiving grant funding or other financial assistance under any federal program," continues the memo.

"Conducting unapproved marijuana-related research could adversely affect the University of Colorado's ability to seek federal research funding or federal financial aid," it adds.

Which means scientists who wish to study marijuana must accomplish the same extraordinary feat as scientists in any other state: obtain approval from the National Institute on Drug Abuse (NIDA).

Only then can researchers gain access to the sole legal supply of marijuana in the U.S., which is grown and housed at the University of Mississippi.

These protocols exist because of international treaties to which the U.S. is a signatory, especially the Single Convention on Narcotic Drugs of 1961, which was the first international accord to prohibit the production and supply of cannabis. The International Narcotics Control Board was put in charge of administering controls on drug production, international trade, and dispensation. The United Nations Office on Drugs and Crime (UNODC) was delegated the Board's day-to-day work of monitoring the situation in each country and working with national authorities to ensure compliance with the Single Convention. From the U.S. code:

> Pursuant to section 201(d) of the Act (21 U.S.C. 811(d)), where control of a substance is required by U.S. obligations under international treaties, conventions, or protocols in effect on May 1, 1971, the Administrator shall issue and publish in the Federal Register an order controlling such substance under the schedule he deems most appropriate to carry out obligations.

Until very recently few cannabis research projects were approved in the U.S. But as shown, Watson and Clarke's HortaPharm was given an official "leave" by the Netherlands in 1994 to do research, and when the permission was not renewed, they were able to continue their research – under conditions that have never been publicly revealed. Even with HortaPharm having unauthorized equipment, and growing way over their limits, they were never shut down. Matter-of-fact, HortaPharm continue to grow. A February 28, 2014 press release by HortaPharm's business partner GW Pharmaceuticals:

GW Pharmaceuticals Receives Orphan Drug Designation by FDA for Epidiolex(R) in the Treatment of Lennox-Gastaut Syndrome

LONDON, Feb. 28, 2014 (GLOBE NEWSWIRE) -- GW Pharmaceuticals plc (AIM:GWP) (Nasdaq:GWPH) ("GW") announced today that the U.S. Food and Drug Administration (FDA) has granted orphan drug designation for Epidiolex®, GW's product candidate that contains plant-derived Cannabidiol (CBD) as its active ingredient, for use in treating children with Lennox-Gastaut syndrome (LGS), a rare and severe form of childhood-onset epilepsy. Epidiolex is an oral liquid formulation of a highly purified extract of CBD, a non-psychoactive molecule from the cannabis plant.

In November 2013, GW announced that the FDA had granted orphan drug designation for Epidiolex in the treatment of Dravet syndrome. Following the successful follow-on offering completed in January 2014, GW intends to advance a full clinical development program for Epidiolex for the treatment of both LGS and Dravet syndromes. Working with leading pediatric epilepsy specialists in the United States, GW expects to commence an initial Phase 2 clinical trial for Epidiolex in the second half of 2014. This trial, if successful, is expected to lead to Phase 3 pivotal trial programs in both Dravet syndrome and LGS intended to support New Drug Applications with the FDA.

LGS is a severe form of childhood-onset epilepsy. Seizure types, which vary among patients, include tonic (stiffening of the body, upward deviation of the eyes, dilation of the pupils, and altered respiratory patterns), atonic (brief loss of muscle tone and consciousness, causing abrupt falls), atypical absence (staring spells), and myoclonic (sudden muscle jerks). Most children with LGS experience some degree of impaired intellectual functioning or information processing, along with developmental delays, and behavioral disturbances. LGS can be caused by brain malformations, perinatal asphyxia, severe head injury, central nervous system infection and inherited degenerative or metabolic conditions. It is estimated that there are approximately 14,000-18,500 patients with LGS in the United States and 23,000-31,000 patients with LGS in Europe.

"This orphan designation for Epidiolex, GW's purified CBD medicine, in Lennox-Gastaut syndrome follows on from the recent FDA grant of orphan designation in Dravet syndrome. We are now in active discussions with the FDA regarding the U.S. regulatory pathway for Epidiolex and believe that this medicine has the potential to meet the significant unmet need of children suffering with severe seizures where all options to control those seizures have been exhausted," stated Justin Gover, GW's Chief Executive Officer. "GW is responding to this need with the goal of providing an FDA-approved prescription CBD medicine that physicians have confidence in prescribing and parents can trust for quality, consistency and access."

About Orphan Drug Designation

Under the Orphan Drug Act, the FDA may grant orphan drug designation to drugs intended to treat a rare disease or condition – generally a disease or condition that affects fewer than 200,000 individuals in the U.S. The first NIDA applicant to receive FDA approval for a particular active ingredient to treat a particular disease with FDA orphan drug designation is entitled to a seven-year exclusive marketing period in the U.S. for that product, for that indication.

About GW Pharmaceuticals plc

Founded in 1998, GW is a biopharmaceutical company focused on discovering, developing and commercializing novel therapeutics from its proprietary cannabinoid product platform in a broad range of disease areas. GW commercialized the world's first plant-derived cannabinoid prescription drug, Sativex®, which is approved for the treatment of spasticity due to multiple sclerosis in 25 countries. Sativex is also in Phase 3 clinical development as a potential treatment of pain in people with advanced cancer. This Phase 3 program is intended to support the submission of a New Drug Application for Sativex in cancer pain with the U.S. Food and Drug Administration and in other markets around the world. GW has a deep pipeline of additional cannabinoid product candidates, including Epidiolex which has received Orphan Drug Designation from the FDA for the treatment of Dravet and Lennox-Gastaut syndromes, severe, drug-resistant epilepsy syndromes. GW's product pipeline also includes compounds in Phase 1 and 2 clinical development for glioma, ulcerative colitis, type-2 diabetes, and schizophrenia. For further information, please visit www.gwpharm.com.

GW Pharmaceuticals, currently, has the first, second and *only* FDA approvals for raw-plant-cannabis-based medicines, using seeds and strains from Watson and Clarke's HortaPharm. GW Pharmaceuticals has a marketing agreement with Bayer AG. A May 2003 GW Pharmaceuticals press release:

> GW Pharmaceuticals plc ("GW") and Bayer AG ("Bayer") have entered into an exclusive marketing agreement for GW's cannabis-based medicinal extract product, to be marketed under the Sativex® brand name.
>
> Bayer has obtained exclusive rights to market Sativex in the UK. In addition, Bayer has the option for a limited period of time to negotiate the marketing rights in other countries in European Union and selected other countries around the world.
>
> The financial terms of this partnership have been established to yield equal long term value to each partner. GW has maintained a significant share of long term product revenues whilst benefiting from a signature fee, an innovative advance working capital facility and milestone payments in the near term to further enhance GW's cash position.
>
> The medicine has been developed by GW to provide a medically acceptable cannabis-derived product for the treatment of the debilitating symptoms of Multiple Sclerosis (MS) and severe neuropathic pain. The product is a whole plant medicinal cannabis extract containing TetranabinexTM (Tetrahydrocannabinol ("THC")) and NabidiolexTM (cannabidiol ("CBD")) as its principal components. The medicine is administered by means of a spray into the mouth.

GW submitted a product license application for Sativex to the UK Medicines and Healthcare Products Regulatory Agency ("MHRA") in March 2003.

Sativex and a THC medicine are also undergoing Phase III trials for the treatment of cancer pain. If approved, Bayer will also market these medicines for cancer pain.

In addition to a share of product revenues, GW has received a signature fee and will receive additional fees on regulatory approval in the UK of the initial indications of MS, neuropathic pain and cancer pain, totaling £25 million. In the event that Bayer exercise the option for countries outside the UK, additional milestones shall be payable on a country by country basis.

Of the £25 million milestone payments, £10 million can be drawn by GW in advance as an interest-free working capital facility to support ongoing preparations for market launch of Sativex. The facility can be drawn by GW at GW's discretion until MHRA approval is obtained. On approval, Bayer has the option to convert the facility into a milestone payment or to convert into GW shares at an agreed premium to the share price at the time of conversion. The facility is subject to additional conditions if MHRA approval is not obtained by 30 September 2004.

GW is to be responsible for commercial product supply and has entered into a supply agreement with Bayer. GW will manage the supply of product through a range of contract manufacturing partners, arrangements for which are all in place.

Dr. Geoffrey Guy, Executive Chairman of GW, said: "We are delighted to have entered into this partnership with Bayer. Having recently submitted the regulatory dossier for Sativex to the UK regulatory authorities, this announcement is a further significant achievement for GW. It is GW's first commercial collaboration and marks the start of a new phase in the company's history. As a leading global pharmaceutical company, Bayer is well placed to maximize the market opportunity for GW's product."

Commenting on the commercial terms of the agreement between the two companies, Dr. Guy added: "GW's commercial strategy is to maximize the value of its products by entering into agreements at a late stage of development. The terms of this agreement reflect the merits of this strategy. Most importantly, GW retains a significant interest in revenues from product sales."

Dr. Christa Kreuzburg, Head of Europe for Bayer Health-Care's Pharmaceuticals Division, said: "We are delighted that GW has selected Bayer as its marketing partner to bring this innovative medicine to market. Supporting medical professionals with effective therapies for the management of MS and severe neuropathic pain is an area of largely unmet need. I am therefore very excited that Bayer will be bringing a product to market with the potential to make a significant contribution in this area. Our two companies are now working closely to prepare for market launch in the UK. Sativex will enhance our portfolio in the UK extremely well and strengthen the market position of Bayer Pharmaceuticals."

Bayer AG is a German chemical and pharmaceutical company founded in 1863. Its first product was aspirin, and it began marketing heroin in 1895. After World War I, its North American business was confiscated by the U.S. government and later acquired by Sterling Drug. The rest of its world-wide enterprises, became part of IG Farben. After World War II, the Allies broke-up IG Farben, and Bayer AG reappeared. Bayer AG re-acquired its North American franchise in 1994, and the brand rights to Bayer Aspirin. Bayer AG does $13 billion annually in the U.S., and about $55 billion world wide. According to Contract Pharma's 2013 report, Bayer AG is the fourteenth largest firm in the pharmaceutical industry. Definitely a player in "Big Pharma."

Is the HortaPharm-GW-Bayer triumvirate a long-term operation to patent and monopolize cannabis' medicinal qualities, concentrating on particular plant strains? Will the forensics developed by HortaPharm be used to track strains, and eventually, to claim ownership of certain strains? And how and why was HortaPharm allowed to continue their work without proper certification? How did the Netherlands get around the United Nations Office on Drugs and Crime (UNODC)? The UNODC, established in 1997, oversees the international treaties, establishes protocols, gathers data and releases annual reports on the illegal drug trade.

The *2006 UN Drug Report* has a report about sinsemilla marijuana that includes an interesting paragraph and footnotes:

Experiments crossing sativa and indica strains led to the development of "skunk," a hybrid said to be 75 per cent sativa and 25 per cent indica, which was among the first to capture the THC high of the sativas with the rapid growth cycle and yield of the indicas.[97] It remains one of the cornerstone cultivars used in contemporary breeding, and in countries such as Australia, France, New Zealand and the United Kingdom, cannabis with a high THC content is often referred to as "skunk" today.[98]

Footnote 97 states:

Preston, B (2002) *Pot Planet*. New York: Grove. p. 154. This account was confirmed by informants in[*sic*] active in early cannabis breeding scene in interviews with the author in Amsterdam in November 2004.

When you check *Pot Planet,* page 154, you find:

[In the mid-eighties an anonymous American, now]referred to as Skunk Sam or the Skunk Man, brought to Amsterdam the first wave of American marijuana genetics. He shared his knowledge and his seeds primarily with Ben Dronkers of Sensi Seeds and Eddie, owner of the Flying Dutchmen Seed Company, who remembers, "He was really into seeds, I mean like nobody else was at that time, maybe a few people on earth, and he took a whole lot of seeds here, different strains, and things really happened fast. The old Dutch outdoor grass was forgotten and everyone went with the new genetics. It was the Great Leap Forward."

Among the strains he brought over were the Colombian ancestor of the sativa Haze strains, and a few crosses of his own, among them an infamously stinky, 75 percent sativa, 25 percent indica, Colombian-Mexican-Afghan cross called Skunk Number One ...

So who are the informants, and are they informants in the police sense of the word, or are they simply giving information to the author of the UN Drug Report? Are the informants the Dutch seed merchants, or are they Watson and Clarke? Notice also that *Pot Planet's* history completely forgets about Nevil Schoenmaker and others. But a bigger question is how does one get to travel in such august official circles? Who greases the skids so that a "busted" pot grower trucks with high official muckety-mucks?

Watson, in March 2004, wrote in a forum as Sam_Skunkman:

> G13 [cannabis strain] is not from University of Miss, I have been to the facility, I was invited to visit by Dr. ElSohly ....

According to a 2012 *USA Today* article, Dr. Mahmoud ElSohly had been "the head of the marijuana research program since 1981." He is listed as a Research Professor in the Research Institute of Pharmaceutical Sciences and a Professor of Pharmaceutics. The marijuana growing project is part of the University of Mississippi's School of Pharmacy, and is currently known as the National Center for Natural Products Research. From the NCNPR's website:

Mahmoud ElSohly

> The National Center for Natural Products Research (NCNPR) was created to bring together *an alliance of academia, government, and the pharmaceutical and agrochemical industries to integrate research, development, and commercialization of potentially useful natural products.* It is the nation's only university-affiliated research center devoted to improving human health and agricultural productivity through the discovery, development, and commercialization of pharmaceuticals and agrochemicals derived from natural products. [Emphasis not in original.]

Dr. ElSohly also profits from the Drug War. He runs ElSohly Laboratories, Incorporated (ELI), a privately held corporation registered with DEA and FDA, which has been offering services to the drug testing community since 1985. The company performs testing for drugs of abuse, and reference analyses for commercial and governmental clients.

Watson's good friend and "benefactor" James Goodwin aka Mel Frank, grow book author, has noted a long time relationship with the University of Mississippi's pot program:

> **Mel Frank:** I think it was in, must have been '81 that I got a call from Carlton Turner, who was the head of that [U. of Mississippi marijua-

na farm], and later became Reagan's advisor on drugs. Not a bad guy, I must admit; he did testify before the political bureau in Mississippi about decriminalizing marijuana and lessening the penalties, so anyway for possession. He actually later quit the Reagan Administration because of the drug policies, but he called me up one day.

"Listen here we have been hearing about this sinsemilla stuff, right, this sinsemilla stuff, supposed to be really strong, and best stuff we had here tested at 6.5% THC, and it came from Humboldt County." And he asked if I could round some of that up for him. Get him some seeds.

I said, "Sure Carlton." He's calling me up; it's like January or February obviously there is nothing growing then [laughs] so I just went to my last years' harvest from my greenhouse, and what I used to do was grow all these different varieties and I would seed a branch or selected buds on each plant and then over the winter I would smoke that with a number of friends, I would give them numbered joints, and they would give me a report on the quality and the high, and then I would select one.

Marijuana Man: Good to be a friend of Mel's.

Mel Frank: One from that, one mother I would plant from that variety for the next year, and that was how I went about my breeding program and it was incredibly successful, that simple way was very successful, so all I had was the seeds and the dregs from buds that the seeds came in so I rounded up a bunch of that stuff and sent it to him with a series from a Mexican variety that I had taken a different sample from each week because I wanted to trace the THC rise and fall, so I never told him that I just included that right in there, and he gave me a report on that.

First of all he [Turner] called me up one day and he said "Is this uh, you can vouch for all this right? You can vouch for all this stuff?"

I said, "What do you mean vouch for this, what do you mean?"

Well he says, "None of this stuff has been adulterated right? Theres no hash oil or anything like that in any of this stuff right?"

I said, "Oh no absolutely not, I can vouch for every single one them, its all just, its all just seeded buds.

So, "Okay," he says.

So I ask, "Why?"

"Because some of these are testing really high."[1]

1   https://www.youtube.com/watch?v=qvkcfrcXmMM&feature=player_embedded

Wow, quite the conversation between an "outlaw" grower and the nation's "Drug Czar." Let's see what Jack Herer in his classic, *The Emperor Wears No Clothes* (Eleventh edition, 2007), had to say about "not a bad guy" Carlton Turner:

Official Corruption: Carlton Turner

In all the research this author has done about the misapplication of public funds and trusts, nothing, it seems, compares with the either totally ignorant or willful manslaughter of fellow Americans by the bureaucrats and politicians of the following story:

One Man & His Drug Scams

The U.S. government policy, starting in the Nixon and Ford administrations and continuing under Carlton Turner[2] (Drug Czar under Reagan 1981-1986), allowed federal medical marijuana, supplied to the individual state marijuana medical programs, to consist only of the leaf of the marijuana plant, even though it's usually only one-third as strong as the bud and doesn't contain the same whole spectrum of the "crude drug," i.e. the THC and CBNs.

For example, the leaf's relief of ocular pressure for glaucoma patients is much shorter lasting and therefore unsatisfactory, compared to the bud. Also, the leaf sometimes gives smokers a headache. The federal government until 1986 used only the leaf. Turner said to the pharmaceutical companies and in interview, that leaf is all Americans would ever get – although the bud works better. Still today in 2007, the five legal marijuana users in the U.S. only get leaf, branch, and bud chopped up and rolled together. Although buds work better for chemotherapy, glaucoma, etc., the branches can be as toxic as smoking wood.

Turner said, in 1986, that natural marijuana will "never" be given as a medicine and, as of April 1998, it still hasn't. (Except in

---

2   *Prior to becoming Special White Hose Advisor (read: National Drug Czar) Carlton Turner, from 1971 to 1980, was the head of all U.S. government marijuana grown for drugs by reason of his position at the University of Mississippi. The U. of Mississippi Marijuana Research Program is *directed by state charter to discover – initiate or sort out the constituents of THC – a "simple" crude cannabis drug that works as a medicine – then synthesize the substances with beneficial medicinal properties to attain their full potential for pharmaceutical companies.* [Emphasis not in original]

California, where citizens successfully voted, in November 1996, to overrule the federal government on medical marijuana!)

The reasons given:

• Buds are too hard to roll through a cigarette machine. (Forget the 25 million Americans who do quite well at rolling bud everyday.)

• *By extracting compounds from the "crude drug" of the bud, there would be no pharmaceutical patents, therefore no profits. Therefore, his program would have worked against his former employers, the Mississippi University's legislative charter and funding.* [Emphasis not in original.]

> (Interviews by Ed Rosenthal for *High Times* magazine; Dean Latimer, et al.; National Organization for the Reform of Marijuana Laws, or NORML.)

Although buds work better for chemotherapy, glaucoma, etc., Turner said they will "never" be given.

It also became evident the famous marijuana "munchies" (appetite stimulation) were not working for the cancer chemotherapy patients using federal leaf.

And even though no studies have been allowed to compare leaf with bud, we know of doctors who unofficially recommended bud and watch their wasting cancer patients put on weight (NORML).

Poisoning Pot Smokers

In August and September, 1983, Turner went on national television to justify the illegal marijuana spraying (by plane) of paraquat in Georgia, Kentucky, and Tennessee by the DEA. He said it would teach a lesson to any kid who died from paraquat-poisoned pot.

Turner was forced to resign after announcing his conclusions in public that marijuana caused homosexuality, the breakdown of the immune system, and, therefore, AIDS.

Looking into the therapeutic potential of cannabis is the most controlled and discouraged research, but any tests pursuing negative or harmful effects of cannabis are promoted. Since these tests often backfire or are inconclusive, even this research is rare.

Turner quoted "The Decline and Fall of the Roman Empire" to show how jazz (rock) singers are eroding the America "he" loves with this hallucinogenic drug – marijuana! Which he meant to stamp out.

Phony Paraquat Kits

During the 1978 Mexican marijuana paraquat scare, and while still a private citizen working for the state of Mississippi marijuana farm, this same Carlton Turner called *High Times* magazine to advertise a paraquat tester.

Unknown to Turner, *High Times* was not accepting ads for any paraquat testers because all evidence showed the testers didn't work.

Dean Latimer – then a *High Times* associate editor, strung Turner along in virtually daily phone conversations for a month, listening to Turner talk about how much money Turner was going to make from sales of the device.

High Times wanted to see a sample. When Turner delivered his prototype version of the paraquat test kit to *High Times*, it was a total "Rube Goldberg" type rip-off, "just like the dozen or so phony kits other companies tried to buy ad space for at this time," wrote Latimer in an article published in 1984.

Turner apparently never thought *High Times* was ethical enough to check the contraption out. He assumed they would just take the ad money and run – print the ad and make Turner rich.

He didn't care if some kid died or was bilked out of money believing in his bogus paraquat test kit.

After this attempted mail fraud, this man became President Reagan's national drug czar in 1981, recommended by George Bush and Nancy Reagan.

A Wanton Disregard For Life

Turner even said that he doesn't even care if hundreds of kids die from smoking pot the federal government has deliberately sprayed with paraquat.

Then at the April 25, 1985, PRIDE conference in Atlanta, Georgia, with Nancy Reagan and 16 foreign First Ladies in attendance (including Imelda Marcos), Turner called for the death penalty for drug dealers.

Turner was, after all, Reagan's, Bush's, and the pharmaceutical companies' own hired gun, who saw his entire mission as not against heroin, PCP, or cocaine, but to wipe out pot and jazz/rock music...

Carlton Turner was forced to resign after *Newsweek* magazine excoriated him October 27, 1986, in a large editorial sidebar. His resignation was a foregone conclusion after being lampooned in the *Washington Post* and elsewhere as no other public figure in recent memory for his conclusions (in public addresses) that marijuana smoking caused homosexuality, the breakdown of the immune system, and, therefore, AIDS.

He resigned December 16, 1986. What should have been front page headline news was buried in the back pages during the Iran-contra scandal that exploded that week.

Urine Testing Company

After his resignation, Turner joined with Robert DuPont and former head of NIDA, Peter Bensinger, to corner the market on urine testing. They contracted as advisors to 250 of the largest corporations to develop drug diversion, detection, and urine testing programs.

Soon after Turner left office, Nancy Reagan recommended that no corporation be permitted to do business with the Federal government without having a urine purity policy in place to show their loyalty.

Just as G. Gordon Liddy went into high-tech corporate security after his disgrace, Carlton Turner became a rich man in what has now become a huge growth industry: urine-testing.

This kind of business denies the basic rights of privacy, self-incrimination (Fifth Amendment) rights, unreasonable search and seizure, and the presumption of innocence (until proven guilty).

Submission to the humiliation of having your most private body parts and functions observed by a hired voyeur is now the test of eligibility for private employment, or to contract for a living wage.

Turner's new money-making scheme demands that all other Americans relinquish their fundamental right to privacy and self-respect.

And Turner's views haven't changed, appearing on Fox News on March 15, 2013, Former Reagan administration drug czar Dr. Carlton Turner said that the health risks associated with marijuana make the question of legalization a dangerous proposition, and he is currently a vocal opponent to medical marijuana on Florida.

Cannabis as a pharmaceutical is nothing new. As you can see in photo, this was how hashish was sold over the counter in the 19th century and prior to prohibition in 1937. On the label one can see its use for anti-spasm. This pure resin was collected from farms in Central Asia for British and U.S. pharmaceutical firms from 1840-1940.

But how do outlaw growers get such connections to government agencies? And all the way back to 1981? What about 18 U.S. Code § 4 - Misprision of felony?

> Whoever, having knowledge of the actual commission of a felony cognizable by a court of the United States, conceals and does not as soon as possible make known the same to some judge or other person in civil or military authority under the United States, shall be fined under this title or imprisoned not more than three years, or both.

Wasn't Goodwin/Frank committing a felony? Haven't plenty of folks been sent to prison, families broken apart, property confiscated, and had there lives destroyed by getting caught growing a few plants? Turner could have been prosecuted for misprision of a felony. Was there some sort of legal agreement/shield?

The NCNPR is an "alliance of academia, government, and the pharmaceutical and agrochemical industries to integrate research, development, and commercialization of potentially useful natural products." Have commercial interests and other forces corrupted the rules to try to bring cannabis under commercial control? Is there a hidden agenda for control and/or domination of parts of the emerging cannabis industry? Can the current march towards full personal legalization be limited and held back by bureaucratic means, until some sort of corporate control is in place? What is going on?

Chapter 12

Potter's Pot Thesis

Our success has been very much down [due] to the help from HortaPharm. If they hadn't existed I'd have had to deal with non-legal entities. As it is, the plants are grown from stock as part of a research programme by the only people in the world licensed at that time.

Our programme is to have clone lines whose cannabinoid production will be either exclusively THC or exclusively CBD. Then we've got others which have no THC but which produce high concentrations of CBC, CBG or THCV: those are other cannabinoids of interest. We'll establish in the clinical trials which are most beneficial for different conditions. We can then go back to our clone library to breed plants which will specifically produce these ratios and use those clones for the mother plant of that line of production. That will also give us very secure plant registration rights.

– Geoffrey Guy, CEO, GW Pharmaceuticals, *Cannabis Culture,* 1999

Below is an excerpt from a December 13, 2013 article at leafscience.com about GW Pharmaceuticals. The Internet has been kind to the cannabis community; offering many websites, forums and opportunities to learn about cannabis, connect with like-minded folk, and catch up on new developments:

> GW Pharmaceuticals, a drug company that specializes in cannabis-based pharmaceuticals, has received early approval on a patent covering the use of marijuana chemicals for treating brain cancer.
>
> GW Pharmaceuticals announced Wednesday [Dec. 11] that it has been issued a Notice of Allowance from the U.S. Patent Office for a patent application involving the use of THC and CBD, the two main chemicals in marijuana, for treating gliomas.

Once a patent application is deemed a genuine invention, the Patent Office sends a Notice of Allowance that outlines the fees involved with final approval.

Specifically, the company provides this description of the patent:

"The subject patent specifically covers a method for treating glioma in a human using a combination of cannabidiol (CBD) and tetrahydrocannabinol (THC) wherein the cannabinoids are in a ratio of from 1:1 to 1:20 (THC:CBD) with the intent to reduce cell viability, inhibit cell growth or reduce tumor volume."

Filed in 2009, GW's patent application lists Otsuka Pharmaceutical as a collaborator and initially claimed the invention of the "use of a combination of cannabinoids in the manufacture of a medicament for use in the treatment of cancer."

However, it's likely that the application was revised since then to be more specific in its claims, including the ratio of THC to CBD used and the type of cancer treated.

Indeed, the use of cannabis and cannabis-derived chemicals to fight a wide range of cancers has long been suggested by pre-clinical research as well as anecdotal reports.

At GW Pharmaceuticals' website there is a research paper posted, a doctoral thesis by David Potter: "The Propagation, Characterization And Optimization Of Cannabis Sativa L As A Phytopharmaceutical."

An excerpt:

Plants are dried and sometimes left for many weeks before processing, by which time the trichomes will have lost much of their more volatile terpene content. Techniques used to make so-called "modern hashish" (Clarke and Watson, 2007) perhaps offer greater opportunities for collecting undamaged glandular trichomes, with more of their secondary metabolites intact. In one method, cannabis material is simply agitated in cold water and the dislodged capitate stalked trichomes collected using sieves. Jansen and Terris (2002) reported that, with a Dutch Government subsidy, this technique had been adapted to make hashish for pharmaceutical research purposes. Separation of capitate stalked and sessile trichomes was not reported. For the remainder of this thesis, the terms hashish and resin are avoided when referring to products made for scientific as opposed to recreational purposes. The term enriched trichome preparation (ETP) is preferred.

ETP or "enriched trichome preparation" is exactly what Reinhard Delp's innovative patent, "Method and Apparatus for Extracting Plant Resins," *does.*

Potter's thesis, with GW Pharmaceuticals support, appears to build an "intellectual" foundation for the apparent ongoing fraud to confuse the origins of, and theft of Delp's patented process. Dr. Potter is currently part of senior management at GW Pharamceuticals, serving as Director of Botanical Research and Cultivation.

As noted before, there is the May 1998 *High Times* article that introduced Delp's invention without mentioning him, while promoted Mila Jansen and her Dutch company Pollinator. And then James Goodwin/Mel Frank published Robert Clarke's *Hashish!,* which completely ignores Delp's new method and promotes Jansen, even though Clarke had seen and experienced Delp's X-Tractor before publication.

Clarke did research at the University of Mississippi federal program. In his 1982 book *Marijuana Botany,* he thanked Carlton Turner for his support. Turner a rabid prohibitionist, knew the value of medical cannabis, and Clarke was a protégé. Clarke's book then gave him stature to influence *High Times* and the cannabis industry. In the 1990s, while the U.S. government was blocking most clinical research on cannabis, the two DEA officially licensed facilities that were doing raw plant cannabinoid  Robert C. Clarke

research, HortaPharm and University of Mississippi, were both associated with Clarke. HortaPharm, in 1997, lost its official license, *but was allowed to operate anyway.*

The paper by Jansen and Terris, "One Woman's Work in the Use of Hashish in a Medical Context," mentioned in Potter's thesis is quite illustrative. It was published in the *Journal of Cannabis Thera-*

peutics Vol. 2, No. 3/4, 2002, pp. 135-143. The editor of the journal was Ethan Russo, MD, who is currently the Senior Medical Advisor at the Cannabinoid Research Institute, a division of GW Pharmaceuticals. Jansen and Terris are identified as "affiliated with the Pollinator Company," but the trappings and subsequent citations of the "paper" are of the scientific genre, giving the work undue gravitas.

An excerpt:

> The Pollinator was the first modern machine to be designed for the production of hashish. The industry was previously unchanged for thousands of years due to the fact that silk screens used for sieving had not been improved until the creation of modern technology. The first Pollinator machines were sold from home, but after a couple of years, I [Jansen]opened a shop as there was a clear demand by many cannabis growers who had marveled at the first public demonstration of the Pollinator machine by Robert C. Clarke at C.I.A. [Cannabis in Amsterdam, a hemp store] Amsterdam, during the 1994 *High Times* Cannabis Cup event. This gave us more time and space to work on the development of methods to improve the technique of pure hashish production, as previously all the testing was done at the kitchen table. It was in this shop where I made my second breakthrough, the creation of the "Ice-O-Lator®," a water and ice method of making hashish.
>
> In 1997, we practiced at home with jugs of water, but had no satisfactory results. The big revelation did not come until we saw the Extractor." Designed in the USA, and manufactured in Yugoslavia, this system tended to break down within 8 months, and was very heavy and expensive. All over the world, people could buy buckets and mixing machines. In the summer of 1998, I sewed my first Ice-O-Lator bags.

Above Jansen "misspeaks," mislabeling the name of Delp's machine as the Extractor instead of X-Tractor, and blurring the machine's origin. They were built in the Czech Republic, not Yugoslavia. And what was the "big revelation" Jansen wrote of? The use of ice water and raw undried plant material – *exactly the innovative process that Delp successfully patented.* She laid off her actions to the machine's bulk, cost and reliability, and her desire to help people.

The next part of the paper by Jansen and Terris spells out Delp's method, confusing his patent, and *laying the foundation for GW Pharmaceuticals to use Delp's process without acknowledging his patent*. In his thesis, Potter presented Jansen and Terris as *the* source for the process, ETP or "enriched trichome preparation," upon which is based GW Pharmaceuticals' products. Again from the article by Jansen and Terris:

This method of extracting the resin glands from the leaf material involved the use of water and ice. Leaf material is placed in cold water (4°C), where it is agitated causing the glandular trichomes to separate from the plant material. Temperature is again of great importance. As the herbal material is agitated in the cold water, hardened resin glands are dislodged more cleanly. Gravity then plays its part as the trichomes sink, and the plant material is left floating on the surface. With the aid of two precise screens (one for the leaf material and the other for the resin) the desirable mature glands and leaf material are separated. One factor that influences the resin glands are ideal growing conditions. Resin glands from plants grown indoors are slightly larger than those grown outdoors, as the plants have more light, nutrients and water. For outdoor growers of cannabis (or older plants where the resin glands have shriveled with drying), I prefer a 187 μ screen on top. This will allow the resin glands to pass through while containing the rest of plant material. A pore sized screen of 62 μ as a lower screen will trap the extracted glandular heads. For growers of indoor plants with larger sized glands, I recommend a top screen of 210 μ and a 77 μ screen for the lower bag.

The Ice-O-Lator process is very simple, quick and efficient. The process begins by hanging both Ice-O-Lator bags (making sure the bag with the larger pore sized screen is on the top of the fine screened bag) in a bucket and then adding the plant material, ice blocks and enough cold water to 3/4 fill the bucket. A temperature of between 2-4°C is set before starting to agitate the plant material and ice.

After twenty minutes of agitation, the water is left to settle for twenty minutes. In this period, the resin glands sink and any plant material rises to the surface. The top bag may then be gently raised out of the bucket, allowing the water and resin glands to drain. Lifting the lower bag out of the bucket reveals the collected trichomes once the water has drained. The inside of the bag is then rinsed with water to collect all the resin glands from the top of the screen. The outside of the bag is the wrapped in kitchen paper and pressed to remove the water. The resin glands are then sufficiently dry enough to remove from the Ice-O-Lator bag.

The collected resin glands are then placed into a metal kitchen sieve and filtered onto paper below. The resin glands are then ready for complete drying, as moisture may quickly lead to a deterioration of quality due to fungal growth. Once the resin glands are fully dried, they can be stored by pressing, or left in granular form. The Ice-O-Lator has proved to be the most efficient method of separation when taking into consideration factors such as time, purity and quantity. In the "coffee shops" of Amsterdam, the hashish made by this process is highly sought, as its potency and purity have become legendary. Ice-O-Lator bags have been sold throughout the world.

The Dutch Government awarded a research subsidy to the Pollinator Company in 2001 for the sole purpose of investigating resin separation methods for use in medical marijuana.

Jansen is currently hailed as the "Queen of Hashish" in Europe. When my book the *King of Nepal*, German edition, came out at the Cannabiz Expo in Cologne in 2004, I met Mila, and she mumbled about being worried about her reputation. I didn't have a clue what she meant, but I do now. Mila as the ice-hash/bubblehash innovator is a myth perpetrated by *High Times* and much of the rest of the cannabis industry.

By now you can realize the scope of the fraud, when you add the pharmaceutical and other "song and dances," it must be over a trillion dollars. The original medical strains that Mother Nature created are now the intellectual property of the U.S. Government, HortaPharm and GW Pharmaceuticals? They have had an almost 45-year headstart. Delp's ice-method patent was held up for 8 years in Europe and Canada, after the U.S. patent was issued in 2000, which gave GW Pharmaceuticals first crack on patenting the medical efficacies of cannabis. At the same time crop eradication works to destroy the true medical strains around the globe, but not before botanists with UN protection come in to take genetic samples and seeds, which then appear to have been sent to HortaPharm for analysis.

Watson and Clarke brag about having the biggest collection of original landrace (indigenous) medical strains in the world. Their bravado may be true, since they appear to have had access to the University of Mississippi's and others' cannabis strains since at least 1982.

The patients in the federal marijuana program were guinea pigs, and are living proof that even the lowest quality pot is good medicine as long as it has the complete cannabinoid profile. You would think the government would process all CBD-rich feral hemp (ditch weed) collected yearly into CBD oil for medicine instead of burning it.

Clandestine research on cannabis appears to have been going on, at least, since 1969 at the University of Mississippi, and since 1990 at HortaPharm. All while a drug war rages in the countries where the original medical strains came from. And millions here and abroad have gone to jail

Cannabis has been used in Laos and Thailand as medicine for thousands of years. I wonder what the Government of Thailand would say if they knew that GW Pharmaceuticals owns the intellectual property rights to genetics sourced in their country? While at the same time the DEA teaches Thai and Lao police crop eradication? In Laos anything over 10 kilos is currently a death sentence, in a country where cannabis has been sold in the market as a cooking herb and medicine for millennia. The same goes for Nepal, Afghanistan, and India. In India cannabis has been used in Ayurvedic medicine, long before the written word.

The British collected cannabis indica resin from central Asia for their pharmaceutical industries up until the 1960s. Cannabis-based medicine is still sold in India by Ayurvedic doctors, as well in Nepal. Prior to prohibition in 1937, a large percentage of prescription medicine were cannabis-based. Pharmaceutical companies such as Parke Davis, now known as Pfizer, Lilly, Merck, Bayer, and many others made their original fortunes from cannabis-, opium-, and cocaine-based medicines. Many veterinarian medicines have been cannabis-based as well, and are still in use by farmers in third world countries today.

The original medical strains sold by HortaPharm to GW Pharmaceuticals, such as Watson's Skunk #1, are a mixture of three types, Mexican, Colombian, Afghani, all of which were better and stronger than the hybrid. No one supports native cannabis crop eradication more than HortaPharm. When botanists are sent into the field to collect wild cannabis strains or old farmed strains, they would inject Skunk #1 seeds. Seed-banks were gifted kilos of Skunk #1 seeds to give away with every seed purchase.

In 2012 Watson put out a graph that showed how the strains sold in coffee shops, dispensaries and grown at home are descendants of Skunk #1, The true origins have been obscured by myth and lies, made gospel by *High Times* and the rest of the cannabis press. Natural cures Mother Nature gave us all, what we have used as medicine for thousands of years of evolution are now the property of GW and HortaPharm?

Biopiracy and The Tale of Turmeric

"Biopiracy refers to the use of intellectual property systems to legitimize the exclusive ownership and control over biological resources and biological products and processes that have been used over centuries in non-industrialized culture."[1]

From Wikipedia:

> **US Patent law**
>
> One common misunderstanding is that pharmaceutical companies patent the plants they collect. While obtaining a patent on a naturally occurring organism as previously known or used is not possible, patents may be taken out on specific chemicals isolated or developed from plants. Often these patents are obtained with a stated and researched use of those chemicals. Generally the existence, structure and synthesis of those compounds is not a part of the indigenous medical knowledge that led researchers to analyze the plant in the first place. As a result, even if the indigenous medical knowledge is taken as prior art, that knowledge does not by itself make the active chemical compound "obvious," which is the standard applied under patent law.
>
> In the United States, patent law can be used to protect "isolated and purified" compounds – even, in one instance, a new chemical element (see USP 3,156,523). In 1873, Louis Pas-

---

1   Vandana Shiva, *Protect Or Plunder?: Understanding Intellectual Property Rights,* Zed Books 2002.

teur patented a "yeast" which was "free from disease" (patent #141072). Patents covering biological inventions have been treated similarly. In the 1980 case of Diamond v. Chakrabarty, the Supreme Court upheld a patent on a bacterium that had been genetically modified to consume petroleum, reasoning that U.S. law permits patents on "anything under the sun that is made by man." The United States Patent and Trademark Office (USPTO) has observed that "a patent on a gene covers the isolated and purified gene but does not cover the gene as it occurs in nature."

Also possible under U.S. law is patenting a cultivar, a new variety of an existing organism. The patent on the enola bean (now revoked) was an example of this sort of patent. The intellectual property laws of the U.S. also recognize plant breeders' rights under the Plant Variety Protection Act, 7 U.S.C. §§ 2321-2582.

In 1995, the *University of Mississippi Medical Center* was granted U.S. Patent 5,401,504 on Use of Turmeric in Wound Healing. The claim covered "a method of promoting healing of a wound by administering turmeric to a patient afflicted with wound." This patent also granted them the exclusive right to sell and distribute turmeric.

In India, turmeric has been "a classic grandmother's remedy," applied to cuts of children as an anti-parasitic agent, used as a blood purifier, and for the treatment of the common cold for generations. It is also used as an essential ingredient in many Indian dishes. Turmeric is a folk remedy, part of people's traditional knowledge.

In 1996, The Council of Scientific & Industrial Research (CSIR), India, New Delhi requested the USPTO to revoke the turmeric patent on the grounds of existing of prior art. CSIR provided documentary evidence of traditional knowledge including ancient Sanskrit text, and a paper published in 1953 in the *Journal of the Indian Medical Association*.

When challenged, the University of Mississippi decided not to pursue the case and transferred the rights to the inventors, two expatriate Indians, Suman K. Das and Hari Har P. Cohly, who filed a response. They pleaded that turmeric powder and paste had different physical properties. In November 1997, the U.S. Patent and Trademarks Office (USPTO) examiner rejected all claims. This was the first time that a patent based on traditional knowledge of a developing country was challenged successfully.

How can scientists in the U.S. file for patents on agricultural and medicinal products with minor innovations from what is traditional knowledge?

The problem lies with the Intellectual Property Rights (IPR) system, under the World Trade Organization (WTO). At the end of the Uruguay Round of the General Agreement on Tariffs and Trade (GATT) negotiations in 1994, IPRs were regulated worldwide under the Agreement on Trade Related Aspects of Intellectual Property Rights (TRIPS). The system was designed for inventions which are formal, such as those carried out in universities and laboratories, or as part of industrial R&D. As of now, the WTO does not recognize technology innovations by farmers, artisans or grassroot innovators, which happen in an informal setup. These form a large part of traditional knowledge.

Additionally, the IPR system is oriented around the concept of private ownership and industrial innovation. That is at odds with indigenous cultures which emphasize collective creation and ownership of knowledge.

When the U.S. introduced IPRs, it accused the Third World of "piracy." The U.S. official stance estimated that royalties lost in agricultural chemicals was $202 million and about $2.5 billion for pharmaceuticals. However, the Rural Advancement Foundation International (RAFI), in Canada has shown that if the contributions of Third World rurals and tribals are taken into account, the roles are dramatically reversed, they estimated: the U.S. owes $302 million in royalties for agriculture and about $5.1 billion for pharmaceuticals to Third World countries.

In 2010 India's Minister for Environment and Forests, Jairam Ramesh, said, "Indian culture is not written, it is in an oral form that is conveyed from one generation to another. But modern society is based on written form."

The Indians set up the Traditional Knowledge Digital Library (TKDL), a collaborative project of the Council of Scientific and Industrial Research and the Department of Ayurveda, Yoga and

Naturopathy, Unani, Siddha and Homeopathy. It uses the tools of information technology and a new classification system to make available traditional medical knowledge to patent offices in developed countries, so that what was known for centuries is not patented by individuals, companies and research organizations as something they claim to have discovered or invented by themselves.

The TKDL devised a modern classification based on the structure of International Patent Classification (IPC) for India's traditional systems: Ayurveda, Unani, Siddha and Yoga.

This knowledge, found in Sanskrit, Tamil, Malayalam, Kannada, Arabic, Persian and Urdu texts, was inaccessible and incomprehensible to most. The focus of TKDL was on breaking the language and format barriers by scientifically converting and structuring the available traditional knowledge.

This knowledge culled from the ancient Indian texts has been translated into Japanese, English, Spanish, German and French.

Will cannabis' folk medicine history help in keeping the plant available, or will the boys from the University of Mississippi put pot in a bottle that you may only purchase from Big Pharma?

Interestingly, as this book was about to go to print, I received a email from "Robin," which said, "I may have some info about the DEA & IRS, who had a secret meeting in Chicago in regards to the info you had in your book.… If you want to know more, you can call me.…"

Well, I gave him a call, and this is what he had to say. He was a state-licensed medical grower and had attended a family function. There he began chatting with an uncle who served in a three-letter agency, and had just returned from a "secret" meeting in the Midwest. As the drinks flowed his uncle became more talkative. He said that in attendance were agents from IRS, DEA, FDA, Big Oil, Big Pharma, and other government officials, including the sitting Governor of Michigan.

They were gathering together to join forces in an attempt to control the medial marijuana business, and had a plan to accomplish that task within five to seven years. Michigan and Connecticut were to be test cases for their plan. Was this info valid? Who knows? In court it would be called hearsay.

I did look at the Michigan and Connecticut medical marijuana programs, and found that the Michigan governor had just recently, December 30, 2013, signed a medical marijuana bill, which for the first time created the legal classification: "pharmaceutical-grade cannabis," which will be sold only through state licensed pharmacies. And, the "licensed facility shall irradiate all pharmaceutical-grade cannabis ... before delivering that pharmaceutical-grade cannabis to another person."

"It's time to get marijuana out of houses and put it somewhere else," Michigan state senator, Rick Jones said. "Let the pharmaceutical companies grow it and sell it in pharmacies."

Patients and caregivers enrolled in the state's medical marijuana program, enacted by voters in 2008, would still be allowed to grow and possess medical marijuana under current state law. Those who want the "pharmaceutical grade" medical marijuana would have to surrender their existing medical marijuana cards and could no longer grow their own.

Anyone wishing to manufacture, distribute, prescribe or dispense marijuana would have to obtain a license from the Michigan Board of Pharmacy.

In May 2012 the law signed by Connecticut's Governor Dannel Malloy, requires a *licensed pharmacist on site* to dispense cannabis. And interestingly enough in both states, there has been much bureaucratic foot-dragging and political problems in establishing their quasi-legal medical marijuana dispensaries that still conflict with federal law. Plus there is the federal hindering of financial and other operational aspects of a now "legal" business. Stalling for time?

But isn't the game over, with Colorado and Washington legalizing recreational use of cannabis? Or could the federal government try to put the genie back in the bottle? Trumping the people's will and actions for freedom, in favor of overreaching governmental control and profit for commercial interests?

Chapter 13

Going Dutch?

The 2006 UN World Drug Report is produced by the Research and Analysis Section of the UN's Office on Drugs and Crime. These reports are produced annually, full of commentary and data, and are consider to be the "final word" on worldwide drug data and contraband strategy. From the report:

> In addition to improved breeding and the rediscovery of sinsemilla, the movement towards indoor cultivation has also allowed the application of greenhouse technology to what had traditionally been a field crop.[106] Around 1985, some cannabis breeders from the United States fled for a country with more amenable drug policies – the Netherlands. At the time, indoor cultivation of cannabis was just starting to take off in the Netherlands,[107] and the fusion of American breeding stock and Dutch agricultural practice sparked a revolution in cannabis breeding and production.[108] Today, Dutch 'seed banks' sell the product of this breeding over the Internet....

Footnote 107 is interesting, in that it acknowledges that growers have not always received proper grow information:

> There have also been a number of technological innovations that have lost currency. The use of carbon dioxide enriched environments to boost yields has largely been abandoned, due to the greater importance of good air circulation in the hot and humid environment of an indoor grow. The use of 'feminised' seeds, produced from hermaphroditic mothers, has also lost popularity, as the risk of further hermaphrodites (and thus pollen contamination) is a threat, and it is much easier to work with female clones.

Here the UN outlines two frauds, feminized seeds, and the use of CO_2 in indoor grows. Parts of the cannabis industry have bilked the consumer for decades through a strong influence, large advertising dollars, in the marijuana magazines. For over thirty years "zombie" growers have been using CO_2 in grow rooms, which only created atmosphere for bugs, mold and mildew, which of course the industry created products for.

Cannabis is a dioecious plant, having the male and female reproductive organs in separate individuals. So when you feminize seed with chemicals, the males become females the females become males, you still have to sex them, and they are now sexually confused plants. They never reach their true potential. This is applying Monsanto technology to cannabis seed in the hopes of making everyone a seed junkie: one seed, one plant. As well as lowering the overall quality – the plants are sterile. Folks complain that the weed today gets them high for about 30 minutes, looks great, smells great, but no bang for your buck.

Take 100 naturally occurring seeds: half you grow out normally separating the males from the females, the other half you feminize chemically, but you still have to sex them. When you grow the females out using the same nutrients and following same growing procedures, the naturally-grown seed produces finer, stronger cannabis, with anywhere between 30-50% more quantity and THC, with a longer lasting effect. I tried to publish an article showing these test results but no magazine would touch it, I think because of Dutch marketing influence. They sell these seeds as 100% female, but you still have to sex them – separate the males from ladies? Are people that stupid? No, they have been brainwashed; logic has nothing to do with it.

The 2009 THC Expo brought Dutch marketing hype to Los Angeles, where feminized seeds auto-flowering strains were introduced and further reduced the quality of cannabis in the U.S.

Auto-flowering strains are strains bred to edible hemp seed strains which have reduced potency 50%. Which is why much of the weed produced today is not medical quality.

E. Small and H. D. Beckwith. 1979. In *The Species Problem in Cannabis*. Toronto: Corpus Books, p 121-127:

Abstract Twenty-five sets of F1 hybrids [an F1 hybrid means the plants grown from the seed of a cross pollination between types], mainly between "drug strains" of Cannabis (those in which the resin is chiefly of tetrahydrocannabinol[THC]) and "non-drug strains" (those in which the resin is composed chiefly of cannabidiol [CBD]) were examined. The majority of these were chemically intermediate between their respective parents, showing no dominance toward either parent.

[So, in the plants grown from the resulting seed (the "F1" generation), THC went down with respect to the "marijuana" parent and up with respect to the "hemp" parent. The converse was true of CBD.]

Discussion:

... It appears that generally crosses between drug strains and non-drug strains produce plants of intermediate potency.

... [In studies of drug strains...] The importance of protecting the [genetic] stock against contamination from pollen by non-drug strains is stressed by the fact that the amount of THC may be halved in hybrid plants.

What these authors don't go on to discuss is what would happen next, in practical terms.

We know, then, that the first generation has been degraded by half. If that "mixed-blood" seed is grown hidden again among hemp plants that will again provide the pollen, then the next generation will again lose by half, gradually by this means (it's called a "back-cross" by plant breeders) converging toward the hemp type. But it is unlikely it would get that far, as the material would be undesirable after the first contamination.

This is why marijuana growers want to stay away from hemp and an example how the Dutch marketing scam lowers the quality of weed using hype advertising in *High Times*, *Skunk* magazine, *Treating Yourself*, and others. Lowering the quality across the U.S., ruining crops due to hermaphrodites, which seed your crop.

A Day in the Life

Ben Dronkers has two museums, one in Amsterdam and one in Barcelona: marketing tools for the Dutch hype. He is banking that future generations will never be able to get imported hashish, nor be able to travel to hashish producing countries to judge for themselves.

Ben Dronkers & Ed Rosenthal

Dronkers owns multiple seed banks, including the venerable Sensi-Seeds. Advertising in the trade magazines, many simply sell the same seeds, but with different names. A bulk of the "Dutch" seeds are produced in Spain. Ironically, there is a museum in Barcelona promoting the Dutch way, when cannabis was first introduced into Spain by the Phoenicians 1500-300 BC.

Every step forward Dronkers has made has been at the expense of others. He was Nevil's Dutch distributor for his seeds up until the time of Nevil's arrest in Australia in 1990 on an international warrant from Operation Green Merchant.

Nevil thought he could keep his business going while in jail, but Dronkers stopped his seed distribution, forcing Nevil in a corner. Nevil eventually sold his seed bank business and the Cannabis Castle to Dronkers.

It's as if the Dutch declared a year zero for cannabis, and everything since 1990 has been the Dutch way, with the guiding hands of David Watson and Robert C. Clarke. Clarke stays the academic, while Watson has three personalities: outlaw grower, scientist, and licensed DEA cannabis grow facility owner. With Ed Rosenthal and James Goodwin aka Mel Frank as the industry's grow-guru gnomes

Worldwide, the cannabis industry has been dumbed down, taught "learning curves" for profit that make no horticultural sense. Thirty years of cannabis grow books later, and you have a generation of zombie growers, who have been taught wrong techniques: ones that artificially inflate the price of cannabis.

When Colorado opened up, the Dutch were there teaching their methods. If you go today, most every infusion company in Colorado is using the bag resin-extraction technique, which destroys trichomes and dilutes the final product. They market their products as medicine, when much of the medicine has been lost in the process.

James Goodwin/Mel Frank, the publisher of Red Eye Press, once stated: everything Ed Rosenthal knew about cannabis or hashish, he learned from Robert C. Clarke. Rosenthal collaborated with Frank on his first grow book in 1978. Rosenthal calls himself a horticulturist, yet he has no degree. He teaches horticulture and has written a textbook for Oaksterdam University. It was the hand of Rosenthal who came up with indoor lighting schedule. Ed promotes hype. Funny is listening to Oaksterdam Graduates talk so knowledgeable about growing cannabis, when they were never taught photoperiodic control, which is taught in first-year Horticulture 101, standard practice in flower industry for 150 years. In many plant species, the duration of the daily exposure to light (photoperiod) provides cues that help adjust flowering time.

James Goodwin/Mel Frank & Ed Rosenthal

In the U.S., indoor grows use $6 billion in energy consumption yearly. Over the course of 30 years that comes to $180 billion. If photoperiodic control would have been taught, that thirty year energy consumption would have been only $45 billion. The other $135 billion could have stayed in growers' and consumers' pockets, and that's just in the U.S. Growers and consumers were taxed and they did not even know it.

Fewer hours of lighting are required if the dark period is interrupted in the middle of the night. The light break in the middle of the night restores pfr phytochrome level, and since neither of the two dark periods before or after light break is very long, the pfr level does not diminish sufficiently to permit flowering. Properly lit plants stay in vegetative state, and grow bigger and better with tight nodes. This is according to Nelson's *Greenhouse Operation & Management*, a college horticulture text book.

In Southern Oregon growers using 18/6 [18 hours light/6 hours dark] schedule in their greenhouses were using as many as ten 1,000 watt light bulbs in a 1,000 square foot greenhouse to replicate the schedule promoted by Rosenthal and others, when all they needed was a 250-watt light bulb to interrupt the dark period for one hour, which keeps the plants in vegetative state. Electric bills of one thousand dollars monthly, and the greenhouse stood out like infra-red beacons, shining night and day for law enforcement.

That is why I call these folks zombie growers. They slovenly follow Rosenthal, Jorge Cervantes, and every grow book written in the past 30 years, without ever picking up a true horticulture book. If agricultural businesses went by the cannabis industry's grow books, your Mother's Day bouquet would cost you $3000, and a hothouse tomato would cost $100 a pound to produce. This type of advice has artificially inflated the price of can-

Most experts describe Cannabis as a short day plant. It flowers in the autumn, when the photoperiod drops below 12-13 hours per day, depending on the variety and its geographical origin. Actually Cannabis is best described as a long-night plant – interruption of the dark periods by a short light period will completely prevent flowering, while interruption of the light period by even long dark period will not prevent flowering.
– Robert Connell Clarke, *Marijuana Botany* (1993)

There is no such thing as *marijuana* botany: one planet, one botany. In *Nelson's Greenhouse Management & Operation*, a first-year horticulture college textbook, lighting information is a full chapter. But all Clarke devotes to the biggest tool in growing flowers is one small confusing paragraph.

Cannabis is grown no differently than mums or poinsettia. It needs a shorter day and longer night to flower, which immediately makes a 12 hours on/12 hours off flowering program completely wrong. That schedule confuses the plant by leaving it on the fence.

Once the plants get under 11 hours of daylight they start to flower in the longer night. Leaving them on the fence only wastes electricity consumption. Clarke's 18 hours on/6 hours off vegetative time is also wrong. You would need two suns to replicate this outdoors.

Using photoperiodic control you can easily cut five hours of electricity consumption, and with other photoperiodic control techniques even more. It cuts down on the vegetative cycle. Your plants grow bigger faster, and using the times of 10 hours on/14 hours off, they go into flower immediately. Your plants are happier and use less nutrients. It cuts your production costs 75-90%.

Marijuana Botany, by teaching questionable techniques, has helped created a whole industry that artificially inflates cannabis prices, stresses plants and lights up cannabis growers for law enforcement.

nabis and cannabis seed. Clarke's book, *Marijuana Botany* helped start the hype.

An example of a zombie grower: A young stoner bragging about the feminized seeds he bought in Holland, 100% female seeds. After he sexed them? He got 45 females and 55 males, when I pointed out that the seeds were not 100% female, he screamed at me and showed me the packaging that stated 100% female, though he admittedly got 45 females and 55 males? Logic never came into the picture.

Jorge Cervantes is a pseudonym for George Van Patten, a Pied Piper of misinformation. His whole chapter on making hashish is complete hype, all it does is sell nylon bags. Major players in the industry, know that generations born after 1990 would not know what real hashish was, nor was it possible for them to travel the hippie hash trail to see how hash was made traditionally. A new product was created called bubble hash, based on Delp's Ice-Water

Van Patten as Jorge Cervantes

Method, and then attaching the Lebanese dry sieving technique to it in order to sell nylon at wedding-dress prices. Adding the sieving technique to the ice method is sort of like tying mules to a rocket and expecting it to go faster.

The Lebanese use three screens in their making of their famous red and gold hashish.

The industry uses folks like Van Patten/Jorge Cervantes to spread misinformation translated in every major language. Van Patten also calls himself a horticulturist, yet has left photoperiodic control out of his grow books, though it is taught in first year horticultural courses and has been standard practice in nursery and green houses since the 19th century.

Both Van Patten and Rosenthal never mentioned photoperiodic control. They taught light schedules for indoor growing that if you had to replicate outdoors you would need two suns.

Again, the power companies get six billion yearly from indoor-grow power consumption in the U.S. alone, meanwhile, they lit every grower up like Christmas trees for law enforcement. That is how the industry serves the drug war, on the backs of people who believed that were being told the truth by the marijuana magazines.

Van Patten is just one of the many Pied Pipers in the Cannabis movement. He at one time planned on bringing to market a fifteen bag hash-making system, which would have diluted the original formula seventeen times. But after I began making noise, several years ago, his bags never came out.

Van Patten, and it seems the rest of the industry, go by one rule: growers will buy whatever they are told to buy simply because the industry controls the marijuana media

The industry responds with personal attacks on me. I have been called a CIA plant, a DEA puppet. I have been characterized as a hater, as being angry and bitter.

How could I break through the hype that the Dutch seed industry has generated? I started my "12-1" photoperiodic-control-growing campaign. First I got my lighting schedule published in *Skunk* magazine, and it appears to be the last time they will publish anything of mine. It threatens their advertisers. I started a "12-1" campaign on Facebook, and the system took off like wildfire. Almost all the grow books state you need at least fourteen hours of light to keep a cannabis plant in vegetative state, my article showed how to keep the plants in this state using thirteen hours, then seven hours, and then I kept them in vegetative state using four hours. It made every grow book ever written wrong.

Rosenthal on Facebook called it a theory. As I have stated before photoperiodic control is taught in first year horticulture classes. It is standard practice in nurseries and across the spectrum of agriculture. Rosenthal is not a horticulturist. Zombie growers who follow Rosenthal think him a hero, while he takes them to the cleaners.

Nobody has promoted the hype more than Ed Rosenthal. He sold our American cannabis culture to the Dutch, and they sell it back to us. There should also be a statue for President Reagan in Amsterdam, because without his drug policies, the Dutch would not be making an estimated $3.2 billion annually from the cannabis tourist trade. The irony being: Reagan's nickname was "Dutch."

CHAPTER 14

Time Will Tell

Two medical varieties, 'Medisins' registered by HortaPharm in the Netherlands in 1998 and 'Grace' registered by GW Pharmaceuticals in the United Kingdom, have so far been awarded plant breeder's rights.

–Robert C. Clarke & Mark D. Merlin,
Cannabis: Evolution and Ethnobotany (2013)

At the 1997 *High Times* Cannabis Cup in Amsterdam, the introduction of Reinhard Delp's innovative Ice-Water Extraction was an historic event that was soon shunted aside by interested parties. Delp had arrived in Amsterdam in early November. Just weeks earlier in the middle of September, Watson and Clarke's HortaPharm had lost its license, but was still operating under circumstances that "cannot yet be made public." And then eight months later in July of 1998, the "details [were] released of collaboration between GW Pharmaceuticals and HortaPharm."

From a 1997 timeline written by Delp:

> During summer '97, a friend was visiting from Amsterdam with his wife and their toddler son. We made the decision to introduce the Ice-Water-Method in Amsterdam. I designed an automatic application, the Xtractor to better demonstrate the method and make it more transparent than the bucket-mixer method I was using before. Mila/Pollinator Co., known to my friend, seemed to be the obvious partner, since they already offered tumblers.... Mila was initially excited about the project and we prepared the introduction together. I prepared the "Xtractor 420" instructions, graph and the "Millennium news"

flyer with the help of freelancing graph artist in Amsterdam, borrowed 25k US$ from an American living in Amsterdam, who I introduced to Mila and arranged a 5% fee from the XTR sales from Mila to him for the loan. A small metal company in Zlin, Czech Republic … was to manufacture the first 50 XTR 420, a stainless version in a lockable wood box. I used a simpler prototype, metal stand and plastic bucket housing for the nightly demonstrations I gave at the Heerengracht before and during the Cup.

Clarke called Mila in her shop, she announced "the new thing" and answered his question about how it works: "With water." He replied with: "Yakk." Mila explained that Clarke was working on a book about hashish for ten years and was about to publish it.

My friend informed me about a request to license the method by an English party. They wanted me to demonstrate the method in a comparison test with a Pollinator. I luckily got a hold of some U.S. surplus top loader washing machines in Germany, and the test was performed in a farm house close to Amsterdam. I yielded more total yield than the tumbler, and only the first ten percent of the dry sifting result was comparable to the "all bubbles" result from the washer.

A meeting was arranged by my friend, and the English party told me that *I would never have to work again, if I gave an exclusive license.* Not only did I stick to the contract with Mila, but I came to Amsterdam to publish to the public, and did not want the method to disappear with a pharmaceutical company. After that, at the end of the Cup week, my friend told me that some guy asked for a meeting with me. We went to a flat to meet … the "guy from HortaPharm." He demanded not to publish ("We can not publish that.") and to my question, "Why?" He answered "It is too strong to handle for the people." [Emphasis not in original]

The ice-water extraction method created a new world for scientists by separating the terpene (essential) oils from the resin glands of the cannabis plant. The very process by which GW Pharmaceuticals produces their enriched trichome preparation (ETP), from which they make Sativex and other products. Watson claims to have helped with development of Jansen's Ice-O-Lator two-bag system, who was under contract with Delp. This began the confusion.

With the two-bag system the consumer loses 30% to 40% of the cannabinoids. Much of the terpenes: the flavor, aroma and high are left in the bucket. Many of the valuable medicinal terpene oils are left behind.

So in the end, *the quality was reduced to the consumer*. Watson has also claimed he helped develop Richardson's Bubble Bags, and the bag count went up to nine, which diluted the original formula even more. Remember the Lebanese only use three screens in their dry sifting technique. And also left out of the instructions was the fact that the extraction bag systems lost the most valuable part of the medicine: that they kept to themselves and GW Pharmaceuticals.

Reinhard Delp was fully aware of the potential of his ice-water method, and the impact its publishing would have. As a California resident he was legally able to use his method with cannabis after the passing in November 1996 of Proposition 215. His intention always was to make his invention available to the public, using the "public" 1997 Cannabis Cup for the introduction.

In a way Delp has succeeded: everybody in the scene now knows about "Bubble Hash," and there are millions of medical patients around the globe using his ice-water method process. Why the name Bubble Hash? At the '97 Cup folks, noted that Delp's hashish bubbled when smoked, similar to opium.

As an old timer, Delp knew Amsterdam from Provo times in the sixties and through the busing, free-market times of the seventies, when Amsterdam was tolerated as a rest and recreation area for the thousands of U.S. military personal stationed in Europe.

Delp retired from the rat race around the globe in the early eighties, at a time when Amsterdam became a metropolis of snitches, where everything goes, but nothing happens without the man. Amsterdam got too heavy. It was a time of "personal, monetary incentives" for law enforcement. As the Dutch "redistribution scandal" in the nineties finally revealed, Netherlands had become the European hub for confiscated contraband: heroin to supply snitches, hash to re-brand and redistribute. Nothing was left to waste. Free-booting smugglers were lured into traps, lucky to get away with their life.

At the 1997 Cannabis Cup, Hager called Delp the "man of the hour" for his invention. The following year, the '98 Cup, Jansen was rolled out as the inventor of the ice-water method. Delp had been pushed aside. His U.S. patent was granted in 2000, but knockoffs were coming into the States from Canada and Europe.

Jansen and GW Pharmaceuticals received government grants and legal support from their respective governments. The Dutch government soon was requiring the coffee shops to categorize "Ice Hash" separately for tax filing. GW developed a contractual relationship with Bayer. *High Times* and other magazines appeared to support the fraud. Pretentious bag salesmen like Bubbleman appeared everywhere, each with its own media blitz.

Delp had to dig in for the long haul.

His European and Canadian patent applications, which had been held up for eight years, were eventually granted in 2006.

By then fortunes had been made.

On April 1, 2009 GW Pharmaceuticals received "confirmation from its licensing partner, Laboratorios Almirall S.A., that it will pay to GW a milestone payment of GBP 8 million [US$12,000,000]."

In May 2009 Delp's companies, grobots.com and icecold.org were busted by the DEA. His businesses and home were vandalized. Company inventory was destroyed and funds were confiscated. Also taken was his collective's seedbank: ten pounds of high quality seeds from landrace strains.

Delp shouldered on, and in August 2009 he wrote to the University of Mississippi's pot program:

To: <ikhan@olemiss.edu>

Cc: Walt Chambliss <wchambli@olemiss.edu>, <iwalker@olemiss.edu>

Conversation: Ice water method for the extraction of plant resins

Subject: Ice water method for the extraction of plant resins

Dear Dr. Khan

Attached is a documentation of a ice water Hops resin extraction using random homegrown Hops flowers and a chemical analysis of the resins by Haas Co..

The solvent free method is based on the specific condition of plant resins and the carrier plant material. While in ice water resins solidify and become brittle, the "contaminating" plant material becomes flexible (dry material after soaking) and stays intact. Besides Hops, the method has excellent results with a variety of plant resins. It became already the dominating method for personal medical use in the field of Hemp use, and is very successful extracting the "oily coating" of Yerba Santa and other "tar weeds."

I am not a professional scientist in that field and gathered my knowledge and experience in very basic private research. I can supply resin samples from several plant species and offer my experience and equipment.

I would appreciate professional cooperation.

Regards,
Reinhard Delp

Delp spoke to the head of University of Mississippi's Biology Department; he was pleased to have a new method offered and asked Delp to send samples. He sent some of a Yerba Santa extract, but never received any response.

On September 14, 2009 the UK Home Office issued a license for GW Pharmaceuticals to investigate the uses of cannabis as a medicine.

> GW Pharmaceuticals, founded by Dr. Geoffrey Guy, has been licensed under the Misuse of Drugs Act 1971 to proceed with a complete pharmaceutical research and development programme into cannabis and its chemical compounds, and in particular into delivery methods other than smoking....
>
> Dr. Guy said, "There is a considerable body of evidence to suggest that cannabis may have a number of medicinal uses: for the relief of pain and spasticity in multiple sclerosis; for pain relief in other neurological disorders, such as paraplegia and neuralgia; as an appetite stimulant in treating AIDS patients with wasting disease; for the prevention of nausea and vomiting associated with cancer chemotherapy; and in the eye disease, glaucoma. But there have been very few systematic re-

search programmes or controlled clinical trials. Our aim will be to establish the medical facts."

The licenses have been issued to enable a full pharmaceutical research programme to be undertaken. In the event of a Product License being granted for a cannabis-based medicine, the Home Office would be very willing to come forward with a change in the controls of the Misuse of Drugs Act 1971 to allow the prescribing of such a medicine.

Here is NIDA's 2014 online answer to the question: Is marijuana medicine?

There has been much debate about the possible medical use of marijuana for certain conditions, including nausea relief for cancer chemotherapy patients and boosting appetite in people with AIDS. Currently, 20 states have legalized smoked marijuana for medical purposes, but the FDA, which assesses the safety and effectiveness of medications, has not approved marijuana as a medicine. There have not been enough large-scale clinical trials showing that smoked marijuana's benefits outweigh its many potential health risks in patients with the symptoms it is meant to treat. Also, to be considered a legitimate medicine, a substance must have well-defined and measurable ingredients that are consistent from one unit (such as a pill or injection) to the next. In addition to THC, the marijuana leaf contains over 400 other chemical compounds, which may have different effects in the body and which vary from plant to plant. This makes it difficult to consider its use as a medicine even if some of marijuana's specific ingredients may offer benefits.

However, THC itself is an FDA-approved medication. Medicines now on the market deliver the benefits of THC without the dangers and unpredictability of smoking marijuana. Scientists continue to investigate the medicinal properties of THC and other cannabinoids to better evaluate and harness their ability to help patients suffering from a broad range of conditions, while avoiding the negative effects of smoked marijuana.

NIDA spokeswoman, Shirley Simpson was quoted by the *New York Times* in 2010: "Our focus is primarily on the negative consequences of marijuana use. We generally do not fund research focused on the potential beneficial medical effects of marijuana."

The are plenty of long, sad stories of universities and other research institutions trying to get permission from NIDA to get some marijuana from the University of Mississippi to no avail. Over the past thirty-five years there have been fewer than twenty controlled trials on the medicinal value of smoked cannabis. In 2007, Judge Mary E. Bittner issued an eighty-seven page ruling that NIDA's monopoly on pot should be revoked and independent research should be allowed. The DEA overturned the judge's decision, continuing the dearth of scientific research in the United States.

Meanwhile GW Pharmaceuticals has had a bit more luck, recently raising more than $100 million in the stock market. From a January 2014 press release:

> London, UK, January 14, 2014: GW Pharmaceuticals plc (Nasdaq: GWPH, AIM: GWP, "GW" or the "Company"), a biopharmaceutical company focused on discovering, developing and commercializing novel therapeutics from its proprietary cannabinoid product platform, announced today the closing of its previously announced follow-on offering on the NASDAQ Global Market of 2,441,110 American Depositary Shares (ADSs) and the full exercise by the underwriters of their option to purchase 366,165 additional ADSs at a price of $36.00 per ADS raising gross proceeds of $101.1 million (before deducting underwriting discount, commissions and offering expenses).

And then in April, GW Pharmaceuticals received "Fast Track" from the FDA for Sativex:

> London, UK; 28 April 2014: GW Pharmaceuticals plc, a biopharmaceutical company focused on discovering, developing and commercializing novel therapeutics from its proprietary cannabinoid product platform, today announced that the United States Food and Drug Administration (FDA) has granted Fast Track designation to Sativex® for the treatment of pain in patients with advanced cancer, who experience inadequate analgesia during optimized chronic opioid therapy.

Sativex is currently in Phase 3 clinical trials for this indication. FDA's Fast Track program facilitates the development of drugs intended to treat serious or life threatening conditions and that have the potential to address unmet medical needs. A drug program with Fast Track status is afforded greater access to the FDA for the purpose of expediting the drug's development, review and potential approval.

According to 2010 study by a British treatment advisory group, the mean cost of Sativex® per patient is estimated at over $6,000 per year, and this does not include medical appointments or the cost of any unsuccessful medical trials. And Sativex  has its problems: its alcohol base has led to the development of painful lesions in the mouth.

Delp started an infringement case in Canada despite a warning from the opposing lawyers referring to the deep pockets of their clients. He finally received some vindication: his patent was upheld in a Canadian court, and he received an injunction and judgment against Green Harvest, a distributor for Jansen's Pollinator Company in Canada. In May 2012, Green Harvest took a $470,000 default judgment rather than discuss the case under oath in open court. As of our print date in 2014, no monies have been paid. And no news articles have appeared in the marijuana press.

Clarke, in his new 2013 full-color college textbook-type 433-page book, *Cannabis: Evolution and Ethnobotany,* from which the quote to open this chapter came, did not inform readers that he was one of the owners of HortaPharm, nor did he mention Delp and his innovative ice-water extraction method.

Imagine that!

Is it getting clear yet?

Chapter 15

Water Hash

In the '60s and '70s water hash was produced in Afghanistan. These hand rolled patties, were processed using the icy water coming from the Hindu Kush mountains. The farmers would process the cannabis traditionally, separating the resin glands from the plant matter, and then would wash the resin glands in ice-cold water which removed the chlorophyll and any plant matter left.

The resin may have started green, but after this process it was golden. This they dried and then hand rolled into patties and further dried. It was dynamite, but sometimes it came with a white mold on the outside. This was the first Afghani I saw in New York, 1968-1969. In 1973 I was working the border between Afghanistan and Pakistan. I was living in the Tribal Zone with my connection Abdul Gaffur Khan. Since the overthrow of the King, Afghan farmers and dealers moved into the Pakistani Tribal area.

For a higher price, I could buy Afghan resin. Anyway I kept a room at Jahn's hotel, and one day I heard my Danish smuggler friends were staying at the Hotel Kyber, so I went to visit. They had some hand-pressed hash, and we took a smoke together. I noticed on the windowsill there was a glass filled with water and resin. My friend explained that they took the over-processed green resin in a glass of ice water, stirred it, and let it sit. The plant matter would float on top and the resin would collect on the bottom. He then skimmed the top and removed whatever plant matter was floating there, then he would pour it through nylon cloth and, wringing out the water, he was now left with a golden ball of hash, which he dried in the hot sun, and then hand pressed for smoking.

Who knows how long this technique was used in Central Asia. It's obviously part of Chinese pharmacopoeia, which separated the resin glands from the plant as medicine over 5000 years ago. Same in Indian Ayurvedic medicine, a practice thousands of years old. They have been using hashish as an anti-spasmodic for thousands of years; they have used cannabis to induce appetite in humans and animals for thousands of years; they have been using hashish for migraine headaches for thousands of years; for pain thousands of years; the list goes on and on.

My point is that when it comes to cannabis, it's mostly rediscovery. Recently a report came out about the effectiveness of cannabis in combination with morphine when treating pain, as if some new discovery. Reality: they were selling cannabis-morphine mixtures for pain 150 years ago. If you think that O'Shaugnessy invented and was the first to create cannabis tincture and market it, you are wrong, Doctors of Ayurveda have been making tinctures as medicine for thousands of years. Instead of using food grade glycerin as I use today, they used honey. This knowledge that O'Shaugnessy got in India, he applied to British pharmacopoeia.

How can they patent genetics or techniques that has been public information for thousands of years? It blows my mind that Mexico, Colombia or Afghanistan have not moved against GW Pharmaceuticals, since the genetics for Sativex came from those countries. How can some Dutch national register Thai genetics, or Afghani? The DEA is the pharmaceutical industries Gestapo?

It really upsets me when folks today claim that the cannabis of today is stronger than weed from back in the day. First of all, the analysis today is completely different from 50 years ago, when they ground up seeds and stems as well as the bud to test. Today you can take 1 gram samples from the same larger bud, take them to three different labs, and guess what? You get three different results. I wish I could debate Patrick J. Kennedy when he states the pot of today is not your grandfathers pot, what a crock. You wish you could smoke a Thai stick, or Hawaiian, or mountain-grown Mexican sinsemilla, which was grown organically and as good as it gets. The coffee shop weed they sell as medicine is a joke. It smells great, tastes great, beautiful flavor, great bag appeal, but only gets you high for 30 minutes. I remember a friend thinking I had dosed him with LSD after smoking his first Thai, or Colombian Gold that got us so high with laughter and joy, that the only thing that could bring us down was Chinese food, and even then we were still high. Today it all tastes the same. Back in the day every producing country had its own flavors, taste and high, but cannabis has been homogenized. It's not as good as the original landrace strains created by Mother Nature.

Cannabis stocks went up ten-fold overnight when Colorado legalized for adult use January 1, 2014. Some folks came from as far as Switzerland to buy the first legal weed. Cannabis is regularly talked about on the news and everyone wants to get in on the ground floor. Washington state legalized in December 2013 and within a few months had received thousands of applications for grow licenses. Wall street investors came and applied for 30,000 sq foot licenses, invested in warehouses, equipment, the whole nine yards, but they never took into account the number of applications submitted. Washington took everyone's dough, issued licenses to all eligible applicants, then re-divided the amount of grow space issued per license. So the Wall Street boys who built facilities for 30,000 square feet were only licensed for 21,000 square feet. Oh well they have money to burn anyway. Hopefully they have learned the most important lesson: when it comes to cannabis anything that can go wrong usually does. What? Prohibition and its effects.

The drug war is a big scam, a Ponzi scheme by the pharmaceutical companies. Prohibition of Mother Nature is a war crime, a genocidal program. They took us off natural medicines and have been giving us chemically concocted copies of what Mother Nature gave us all for free.

CHAPTER 16

The beat goes on ...

On January 1, 2014 cannabis became legal in Colorado. Prohibition is over, hooray, but is it? It's not over till the fat lady sings in Washington DC.

Surprisingly, back in the day, if you flew in from India, or any other cannabis producing country, you got special attention at U.S. Customs when you entered. Today it's having Oregon, Colorado, or California license plates in Texas or Louisiana, or any number of states where draconian laws still apply. While prohibition goes through its death throes in the U.S., the drug war rages in Asia and around the globe. The DEA has trained law enforcement everywhere but North Korea, all the while the pharmaceutical industry patents the original genetics that came from these very countries. In Asia cannabis has been, and is still, used as medicine, food, cloth, oil, thousands of years before written history.

It's nothing new that cannabis can cure migraine headaches, improve appetite, heal pain. My hope is that this book wakes up these countries to the enormous fraud perpetrated on their societies. Growers and consumers are taxed by the status quo at the artificially inflated price of cannabis, caused by 30 years of skewed grow books and misinformation by the tightly controlled cannabis media to the tune of over a trillion dollars, and they did not even know it. Incredible to an old hash smuggler like me.

1840-1940 were the golden years of cannabis, when hemp and medicinal cannabis were legally grown for the industry, and cannabis cultures flourished worldwide.

1940-1990 were the glory years of cannabis: whoever had the best pot, got the highest price. Smugglers scoured the planet finding the finest cannabis still yet available. Cannabis was cheap, plentiful, and of the finest quality, the original medicinal strains.

1990 brought the weed greed era and the advent of Frankenweed GMO cannabis: smells good , looks great, gets you high for about 30 minutes, with little or no medicinal use.

Recently I received my second death threat. Uruguay is the first country to legalize cannabis. HortaPharm and Bedrocan are the only companies that have legal license to export seeds directly to Uruguay's government. HortaPharm offered genetically marked seed that would make it easier to control.

URUGUAY TO TRACK LEGAL MARIJUANA

In December 2013, Uruguay became the first country in the world to fully legalize the consumption, cultivation and distribution of marijuana. Anyone over the age of eighteen and registered in Uruguay's countrywide database is allowed to purchase marijuana over the counter. There are limits to how much an individual or group can grow and buy every month.

The tracking technology is the same used by the South American country to track its beef. An official could scan any plant with something similar to a barcode scanner and get the plant's complete history from "seed-to-sale."

Uruguay's government-grown pot isn't available until the end of 2014, so the genetically marked plants were not on the market when the government released its official rules and regulations for the legal industry at the end of April. They allow growers to have "illegal" plants as long as they're registered with the national database.

Uruguay's track and regulation systems are far more comprehensive than either Washington's or Colorado's, the only two U.S. states to legalize recreational marijuana. Granted, Uruguay's legal marijuana system as a whole is more comprehensive. Colorado currently has a similar radio-frequency tracking system for its commercial marijuana, and Washington plans for a system that tracks it from seed-to-sale.

Neither Washington nor Colorado requires home growers to register their marijuana though, and Uruguay is the only authority that wants to ensure its citizens are smoking only legal marijuana. Colorado and Washington stop tracking pot at the sale, but Uruguay's genetically marked marijuana would make it possible to determine if any sample of marijuana originated from legal marketplaces.

The system may be reassuring to the significant majority of Uruguayans who don't support the legalization of marijuana. A 2013 poll, taken not long before the government passed the legalization legislation in December, showed fifty-eight percent opposed legalization.

Chapter 17

There's somethin' happenin' here

There but for the grace of God, go I.

– attributed to John Bradford

Millions of us have committed multiple felonies because of our relationship with marijuana. This book isn't about the prohibition of pot, but what that prohibition has wrought: a very convoluted past and a murky future, which is nuanced by its outlaw status.

Marijuana has been associated with humankind for millennia. It has been used both spiritually and recreationally, plus as food, medicine, cloth, and scores of industrial uses. Jack Herer's wonderful book, *The Emperor Wears No Clothes*, brought to our attention the political and commercial shenanigans behind pot's prohibition. This prohibition has had nothing to do with our health, our children or our communities. It has been about keeping cannabis out of the legal marketplace, and the creation of a black market that allows "forces in the shadows" to sell plants, often for more than gold. This has created slush funds that have led to an untoward influence over our civic, commercial and personal concerns.

With prohibition comes gangsters, criminals, intelligence agencies, police and their tactics. Part of police tactics presents a choice that most of us hope we never have to face. What do you do when the cops ask for your cooperation: Do you do the time? Or do you talk?

I myself have been presented with that choice several times. My smuggling tales are not secret, and are told in my book, *King of Nepal*. I have spent time in jails and prison, had my assets seized, and lived on the run.

In Pakistan, I was swept up at a hotel, along with other independent smugglers, one of whom then tried to dump his multiple-run-
ner load on me. He told the police that his loads were mine, and informed them that I was an American fugitive. I had been traveling
under a British passport. I told the truth of the matter, including
about another load that the smuggler who had informed on me had
running. He got out of jail on bond and split. I was extradited back
to the States, spent a total of six months in prison, and received five
years of probation.

In 1995 I was invited to debate at the University of Miami on medical marijuana by friends who owned a head shop locally. The panel
consisted of me, Todd McCormick, Elvy Musika, Irwin Rosenfeld,
and a DEA spokesperson Wayne Zucker. I was seated next to the
DEA. I had just been spit out of the Gulag, having been brought back
from Laos, where I had been held by DEA, who didn't bring me back
until after a civil forfeiture trial in Denver, where I lost everything,
even though I had proven that I had made my money legally. But
since I was a disenfranchised fugitive, they took everything anyway.

I had been in Nepal when they said I was in Arizona, a state
where I have never been, buying tons of Mexican cannabis. So if I
was ever angry and bitter, it was that day. I had seen what the DEA
had done in Asia and across the globe. I had seen them turn Afghanistan into a heroin-producing country.

I was in Asia when the change was made from the Golden Tri-
angle to the Golden Crescent. I saw them destroy cannabis cultures
all across South and Southeast Asia. Countries where cannabis had
been legal, where there was no market for hard drugs. There was no
such thing as a Nepalese or Afghani junkie.

Countries were paid off to change their laws. The last country to
do so, where cannabis had been sold openly at the farmers markets
was Laos. They opened a U.S. embassy after seventeen-and-a-half
years, around the same time that they handed me over to U.S. Customs in 1992. They had no case against me, so charges were later
dropped, but all I was left with was two sticks to rub together.

When it came my turn to speak at the panel, I tore into the DEA.
Asking the DEA agent how come heroin and cocaine was 500%

cheaper than when I was the age of the college students attending? I was his worst nightmare, as I was drug war veteran. I was roundly applauded more than once. DEA agent Wayne Zucker steamed. Little did I know that fifteen years later, a picture of me sitting next to him, taken of that debate by McCormick, would be used to call me a DEA puppet. That is one of the ways they have attacked me, trying to kill my voice.

David Watson aka Skunkman aka Sadu Sam has called me "a snitch," "a nut job," "crazy Joe" and many other names. He has also threatened the loss of advertising revenues to marijuana magazines for printing my articles.

I have been public about my concerns since 2006, and the more I look, the more I find. I have been contacted by many folks who have supplied me with information, but are scared because of the influence of Watson and his buddy Robert Clarke. These contacts, among them a major seed bank owner, have asked that we not use their names.

They tell me about marijuana busts in Nigeria, busted drug-rings in Mexico, busted hash-smuggling operations in the States, and others that all lead back to the Cannabis Cabal. They tell me that since its inception, the Dutch seed business has been partnered with law enforcement. They tell me that they have been invited to private parties, during the Cannabis Cup in Amsterdam, where Carlton Turner and Mahmoud ElSohly have been in attendance, and intriguingly some of the new blood that attends soon gets busted. Something is going on.

Now we have Uruguay legalizing marijuana, but only a kind that can be tracked, and currently in Mexico they are finding plants that "have been genetically improved." Something is definitely going on.

And we are all going to have a chance to make a choice. Will we stand up for truly legal marijuana?

From May 2, 2014, AP report:

> Uruguay plans to disseminate clones of government-approved marijuana plants, so that police can test weed possessed by licensed users and ensure that it's bona fide. Possession of mar-

ijuana lacking the genetic markers of approved plants will be criminally punished.

[Uruguay President] Mujica said "it's a complete fiction what they do in Colorado," which licenses marijuana sellers and producers but allows any adult to buy up to 28 grams at a time. In Uruguay, consumers must be licensed as well, and each purchase will be tracked to ensure they buy no more than 10 grams a week.

As an "industry" friend of mine said: The cannabis economy is a pre-determined market and it is led, while hiding economic transformation from those that participate in that market. Look at the cannabis economy as a identified market ... a market that will constantly conflict until those with the capital and regulations along with government protection, tax collection and investor's blessings take it all.

When some say: Cannabis will be legal. Your response should be: For whom shall it be legal for?

Documents

LARRY D. JOHNSON
Attorney at Law
Patents, Trademarks, Copyrights
And Related Matters

Marin County Office:
175 N. Redwood Dr., Suite 130
San Rafael, CA 94903
TEL: (415) 499-8822
FAX: (415) 472-4347

Sonoma County Office:
1214 College Ave.
Santa Rosa, CA 95404
TEL: (707) 578-9333
FAX: (415) 472-4347

Reinard C. Delp
P.O. Box 123
Laytonville, CA 95454

STATEMENT: February 24, 1997

Mailing Date: July 24, 1997

For Professional Services:

Re: METHOD FOR EXTRACTING PLANT RESINS

     Consultation re: Patent Law; Patentability (novelty) search
for METHOD FOR EXTRACTING PLANT RESINS.

     U. S. Provisional Patent Application for METHOD FOR
EXTRACTING PLANT RESINS, including Specification, (informal)
Drawings, Verified Statement Claiming Small Entity Status
(Independent Inventor), Patent Office filing fees, and filing by
Express Mail; follow-up with conference with client.

Total fees and costs	....	$1,272.50
less amount received	....	(1,272.50)
Total due	....	$ 0.00

Thank you.

Reinard Delp's long journey begins with retaining an attorney to file his patent.

US006158591A

United States Patent [19]

Delp

[11] **Patent Number:** 6,158,591

[45] **Date of Patent:** Dec. 12, 2000

[54] **METHOD AND APPARATUS FOR EXTRACTING PLANT RESINS**

[76] Inventor: **Reinhard C. Delp**, P.O. Box 123, Laytonville, Calif. 95454

[21] Appl. No.: **09/380,253**

[22] PCT Filed: **Feb. 24, 1998**

[86] PCT No.: **PCT/US98/03649**

§ 371 Date: **Aug. 24, 1999**

§ 102(e) Date: **Aug. 24, 1999**

[87] PCT Pub. No.: **WO98/36839**

PCT Pub. Date: **Aug. 27, 1998**

[51] Int. Cl.⁷ B03B 7/00

[52] U.S. Cl. 209/17; 209/18; 209/3; 209/4; 209/5; 209/172; 209/172.5; 209/173

[58] Field of Search 209/13, 17, 18, 209/3, 4, 5, 172.5, 172. 173

[56] **References Cited**

U.S. PATENT DOCUMENTS

4,892,938 1/1990 Giovanetto 536/18.5

Primary Examiner—Donald P. Walsh
Assistant Examiner—Jonathan R Miller
Attorney, Agent, or Firm—Larry D. Johnson

[57] **ABSTRACT**

An improved method and apparatus for extracting resin from plant material. Conventionally, plant resins, which are useful in many products, are extracted using chemical solvents, which may alter the extract, and may produce a by-product or residue that may be unusable or problematic. The present invention overcomes these drawbacks by using cold water in a wash process to cause the resins to become brittle, while the remaining plant material becomes more flexible. Separation is accomplished using an extractor (10) having a washing chamber (12) with an open top (14) and a screen filter (16) disposed above a settling chamber (18). A collection bottle (24) is placed below a valve (22), and may include a filter (26) to separate resin particles from the solute. The washing chamber is first filled with cold water and then a quantity of plant material (P) is placed therein, followed by an ice layer (30). An agitator (32) is then actuated to mix the contents to separate the resins. The settled resin is thereafter captured by the filter (26) upon opening the valve (22).

3 Claims, 1 Drawing Sheet

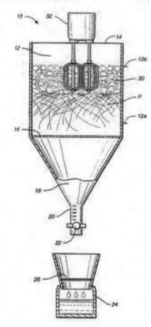

The U.S. patent papers for method and apparatus.

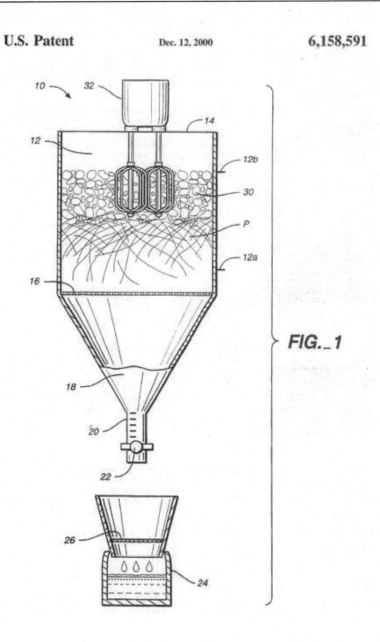

FIG._1

6,158,591

1

METHOD AND APPARATUS FOR EXTRACTING PLANT RESINS

DESCRIPTION

1. Technical Field

This invention relates generally to the processing of plants and agricultural products, and more specifically to an improved method of extracting resin from plant material.

2. Background Art

Plant resins are used in many products. Extraction of plant resins typically involves the use of chemical solvents, which may alter the extract, and may product a by-product or residue that may be unusable or problematic.

DISCLOSURE OF INVENTION

The invention provides a method and apparatus to extract plant resins from plants (including dried or fresh flowers, leaves, stems, roots, and the like) using only cold water in a wash process. The temperature of the cold water causes the plant resins to become brittle, while the remaining plant material becomes more flexible. Separation is accomplished by agitation, filtering the residual plant matter from the resin particles and solution, and then filtering the resin particles from the solution.

The invention provides an "ice-water" resin extraction method which has several advantages. Other than water there are no solvents necessary, resulting in an unadulterated extract which may be of importance in the use of its fragrant properties or as a food additive. The method produces a very clean product in as little as one step, without further filtration through settling for a specific duration. Small fibrous plant particles take time to saturate and settle, while resins fall out sooner. Pesticide residues are simultaneously removed. The plant material from which the resins are removed stays essentially intact for further processing (e.g., steam or vacuum distillation, solvent extractions, etc.) The water soluble components can be separated from the liquid at different levels. Fresh undried plant material can be processed using this ice-water method.

BRIEF DESCRIPTION OF THE DRAWINGS

FIG. 1 is a side elevation view of an apparatus for extracting plant resins of this invention.

BEST MODE FOR CARRYING OUT THE INVENTION

Apparatus or extractor 10 includes a washing chamber 12 having an open (or openable) top 14, with a screen filter 16 disposed above a funnel-shaped settling chamber 18 having a collection neck 20 and a valve 22. Collection bottle 24 is placed below the valve 22, and may include a filter 26 to separate resin particles from the solute, as described infra.

In use, washing chamber 12 is filled with cold water (e.g. 0°–15° C.) to the level of the initial fill mark 12a. A quantity of plant material P is placed into the cold water, and then ice layer 30 consisting of crushed ice, ice cubes or snow may be placed on top of the plant material until the contents of the washing chamber rises to the level of the maximum fill mark 12b. Agitator 32 (such as an electric mixer with stirring whisks) is actuated to mix the contents, preferably in a sequence of mixing and non-mixing (soaking) intervals, to separate the resins from the plant material, as well as to create a solution of that part of the plant material which is soluble into the cold water. After the agitation is stopped, the

2

resins will continue to settle into the settling chamber. The valve may be periodically opened to allow the resin and solution to pass to the paper filter, capturing the resins and allowing the solution to enter the collection bottle. Alternatively, the collection bottle may be directly connected to the valve, allowing the user to fill the bottle with resin/solute for later separation.

In typical dimensions the apparatus is capable of processing plant material in quantities from several grams to approximately 200 grams (dry weight, depending on the plant species). The development of the extractor was based in part on the result of experiments with resin extraction from the flowers, leafs and stems of the *Navarretia squrrosa* (Eschs.). It is a member of the Phlox family (Polemoniaceae). It is a small flower (2 to 20 in.) and is well known for its medical properties to native Americans. The resin is visible to the bare eye and is concentrated on the flowers which are protected by sharp spikes and leaves and stems. It develops during early summer when it smells similar to coffee and changes its odor during ripening to "bacon like". Its strong odor makes it of interest to the fragrance industry.

In the washing or separating process, the container (washing chamber) 12 is filled with cold water to the initial fill mark, which is approximately 1.5" above the screen, to avoid direct contact of the plant material with the screen. After the plant material is placed in the water, smaller fibrous plant particles will absorb water and increase in size before reaching the screen. The plant material will also absorb water and become flexible. Stems are cut to a maximum length of approximately 2". The layer of ice cubes, crushed ice, or snow added on top of the plant material causes it to submerge, accelerating the process of water absorption. The ice will drop the temperature of the water and plant material to a point where the resins become brittle and break off of the surfaces of the agitated, flexible plant material. The separated resin particles are heavy and will drop down to the screen, where the light motion created by the "washing" motion above will wash these particles through the screen. In general a washing time from 30 to 60 minutes will separate more than 90% of the resin.

The screen size is related to the plant species being processed. The gaps have to allow the resin particles to penetrate, and are therefore relative to the specific physical properties of the plant material at cold temperature having been submerged in water.

Due to a buffer effect of the screen the liquid in the settling chamber below the screen is relatively still, and increasingly so towards the bottom. The bigger resin particles roll to the collection neck above the valve. Smaller particles may settle on the inclined surfaces of the chamber (e.g., approximately 45 degree angle), and have to be agitated to further descend, or will be washed out with the final drainage of the chamber. In the case of some plant material after about 30 minutes close to half, and after 60 minutes all the resin separated will have settled. The green to brown color of the liquid is due to water soluble plant components where the lighter essential oils and waxes are in the top layer, or due to undissolved fibrous plant particles suspended in the emulsion. After approximately 10 hours, these particles will have absorbed enough water and descend, clearing up the liquid substantially.

A highly fragrant waxy component can be removed from the liquid by injecting cold water, aerated cold water or fine air bubbles under high pressure causing a layer of foam to appear. This foam when separated (skimmed off) settles to a

6,158,591

3

waxy liquid which is stable at room temperature, unlike the total liquids which start decomposing at room temperature after approximately 24 hours. After separating this waxy compound, the remaining solution may be used as an organic fertilizer as is, or concentrated.

The resin is finally removed from the container through the valve on the bottom and collected in a paper filter, which allows the water to drain. At the bottom layer of the liquid the water separates easy through the paper filter, while the higher levels may have a sealing effect on the filter.

All processes used to wash fabric (e.g., the use of a clothes washing machine) are of use in this method (washing forward, reverse, spinning, rinsing, settling/soaking times, etc.) The specific mechanical movement applied depends on the specific characteristics of the resins and plant materials to be processed. A plant specific sequence can be programmed and automated.

The filter size to separate the resin from the plant material is also plant specific. Resin particles when submerged require a slightly larger screen than dry particles due to their physical characteristics in a water emulsion. A sequence of different filter sizes allows further separation.

Any paper filter with pores smaller than the resin crystals and fragments removes the liquid from the resin. The bottom layer of the liquid can be passively removed from the resin (drip). To extract the resin from the total liquid large surface filters and pressure may be needed. In general, any combination of settling and pressure filtration is possible with the ice-water method.

While this invention has been described in connection with preferred embodiments thereof, it is obvious that modifications and changes therein may be made by those skilled in the art to which it pertains without departing from the

4

spirit and scope of the invention. Accordingly, the scope of this invention is to be limited only by the appended claims and equivalents.

What is claimed is:

1. A method of extracting resin from plant material, said method comprising the steps of:

placing a quantity of water having a temperature in the range of 0 degrees to 15 degrees C. into a washing chamber;

placing a quantity of plant material into the water in the washing chamber;

adding a quantity of ice to the quantity of plant material and water in the washing chamber;

mixing the water and plant material to separate resin from the plant material and to create a solution;

filtering the plant material from the resin and solution; and

filtering the resin from the solution.

2. An apparatus for extracting resin from plant material, said apparatus comprising a washing chamber having an agitator and an open top, with a screen filter disposed above a settling chamber and valve, with a quantity of water having a temperature in the range of 0 degrees to 15 degrees C. placed in said washing chamber, and a quantity of plant material placed into the water in said washing chamber, so that when the water and plant material in said washing chamber are agitated, resin is separated from the plant material and passes through the screen filter to said settling chamber.

3. The apparatus of claim 2 further including a quantity of ice placed in said washing chamber.

* * * * *

```
XTR 's on scedule                          mailbox:/C47C/Program%20...04@euronet.nl&number=114
```

```
Subject: XTR 's on scedule
   Date: Thu, 23 Oct 1997 20:04:19 +0100 (MET)
   From: Pollinator <greenfin@euronet.nl>
     To: Grobots International <grobots@mcn.org>

Hello R.
      Everything sounds o.k. we hope to sell some during the cup, also a
couple of people have already asked to buy the 1000, very exciting, hope to
hear from you soon.
Pollinator
```

Email correspondence from Mila Jansen to Delp prior to 1997 Cannabis Cup.

Amsterdam   November 30,1997

Contract between: Reinhard C. Delp, Laytonville, CA. U.S.A
And
Mila M. Jansen and or Pollinator Company-Greenfingers, DOS#33266193

This contract is a licensing for distribution. It refers to equipment using the Ice
Water Method of separating fragrant plants (U.S. patent pending)

Reinhard C. Delp, owner of the Patent Pending, licenses Mila M. Jansen and or
Pollinator Company for world wide distribution of above described equipment.
For the European Community those rights are exclusive. Those rights are not
transferable and cease if no distribution takes place.

Mila M. Jansen in return pays Reinhard C. Delp 10% of the wholesale price of
above described equipment as a licensing fee.

Amsterdam   November 30,1997

Reinhard C. Delp   Mila M. Jansen
                                            (Pollinator Company)

Typed copy of the Delp and Jansen 1997 contract. Original displayed on page 19.

XTR 420

The buyer agrees to use the XTR at his own risk (or please return UNUSED for full refund).
For one year we will exchange any and all defective parts damaged under normal duty.

Your *XTR 420* is mostly handcrafted in the Czech Republic, each one is individual.
Please handle with care and ease.
To open and close the lid, place lid seams in the back besides the screen insert seams.
Handle vinyl bladder funnel with extra care.

LOADING

Step 1 Connect collection bottle, open valve. Fill the **XTR** to level 1 (see drawing) with (ice) cold water. Check for leaks. (Never bring your plant material in contact with the dry screen).
Step 2 Fill the **XTR** with plant material to level 2 (see drawing), push dry material gently under water.
Step 3 Cover material with a layer of ice to level 3 (see drawing). (For flowers use ice cubes, for leaves crushed ice may be used)
Step 4 Fill with cold water to "run level" (see drawing).

SOAKING AND RUNNING

1) If dry plant material is used, it should soak for 10-30 minutes to become flexible enough to stay intact.
Safely attach the 2 stirring whisks through the **XTR** lid to the mixer.
Replace lid with mixer and connect power.
2) Start the mixer at meduim speed and agitate for 15 minute intervals, allowing 5-10 minute breaks.
Minimum run time: 2 cycles- 30 minutes
(The window allows you to check how much resin is removed)
After approximately 10 minutes the resin will visibly begin to fall out into the funnel chamber and through the open valve into the collection bottle.

SETTLING AND WATER REMOVAL

1) Minimum settling time 30-60 minutes.
After the agitation is stopped, much of the resins will be floating and needs time to fall out, or "settle". During settling time, gently stroke the flexible vinyl funnel, starting at the top to cause the resins to concentrate at the bottom tip (yes, just like that).
2) After the resins are settled, close the valve and remove the collection bottle.
3) Reconnect the collection bottle and open the valve again to collect more resin. Pour off excess water, carefully shaking the bottle and rinsing with cold water, pour the sludge into the paperfilter, let the water drop out

Warmed up, the resin can easily be compacted with hand pressure for multiple use (i.e. aromatheraphy, incense, cosmetics, etc).
When the plant tea is fresh it is excellent for skin care (baths), and later can be used as a powerful organic plant food

TO CLEAN

1) Drain all the water,
2) Remove plant material and rinse with cold water.
3) To separate the vinyl from the stainless for cleaning,submerge both parts in water.

The Instructions that Delp developed and packaged with his first Xtractor, the XTR 420 in 1997. Notice he gives a one year warranty .

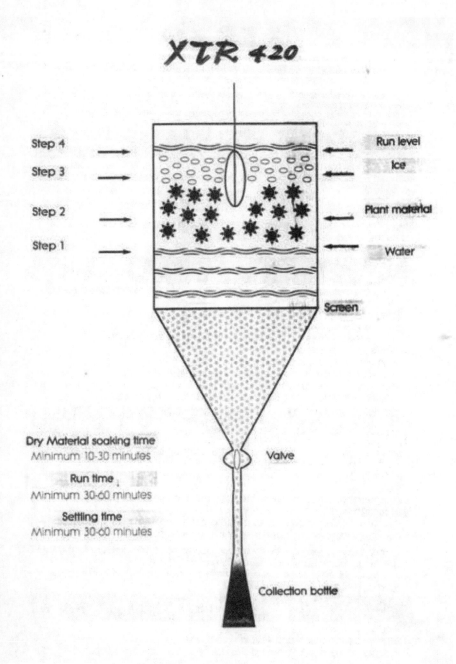

Page two of the 1997 XTR 420 instructions.

ICE-O-LATOR

A   SET UP:
A1 - Buy an electric mixer and a
20 Liter (5 gallon) bucket
that has a tight fitting lid.
A2 - Drill holes in the lid, for the
mixer blades will fit through.
A3 - Fit the inter liner into the
bucket and tighten the cord
around the top lip.

B   LOADING:
B1 - Fill the ICE-O-LATOR to
level 1 with ice cold water.
B2 - Add the plant matter to
level 2 and push dry material
gently into the water.
B3 - Cover the surface with
a layer if ice.
B4 - Fill the bucket with cold
water to just cover the heaters.

C   SOAKING and RUNNING:
C1 - If you are processing dry plant matter, it should soak for 10
to 30 minutes. Soak until it is flexible and no longer brittle.
C2 - Put mixer blades through lid and attach them to the mixer.
Replace the lid tightly. Connect to power.
C3 - Start the mixer a low to medium speed and agitate for 15
minutes, take a 5 minute break, repeat cycle 2 to 3 times!

D   SETTLING and WATER REMOVAL:
D1 - After you stop the agitation, much of the resins will be suspended. They need time to settle! Minimum 60 minutes.
D2 - Once settled, remove the round liner, then stir and pour the
water in the bucket with the resins through the square bag.
D3 - When warmed up, the resin can be easily compacted with
hand pressure for multiple uses (i.e. aromatheraphy, incense,
cosmetics, etc.)

Jansen's instructions for her 1998 Ice-O-Lator that use Delp's design and words.

Swiss Ice Cold, GmbH
Postfach 1017
CH 4502 Solothurn
Switzerland
e-mail @ www.swissice.ch

9/27/99

To Trans High Corporation
235 Park Avenue South, 5th Floor
New York, NY 10003

Dear Friends

The subject might be of interest to you.
Herewith I send you, what I would call: "Chronicle of a rip-off." It is a translation of a response to a German "HANF" magazine article (7/99) in which the newest invention of the Pollinator Comp. A'dam, their " I(ce)- 0- later", is introduced and Robert Ronnel Clarke's book "Hashish" claims origin. Unlike "HIGH TIMES" (see May 98) Clarke doesn't mention our surprise introduction of the " XTR 420" on your Cup 97 in his book. Instead he introduces his own "XTRACTOR" and his own cool water method.....
We thank HIGH TIMES for the excellent journalism and truly independent reporting.

Sincerely,   Swiss Ice Cold GmbH, R. Delp

Two letters Delp sent to *High Times*. He received no response.

Swiss Ice Cold Gmbh
Postfach 1017
CH4502 Solothurn
Switzerland
www.swissice.ch

3/16/00

To Trans High Corporation
235 Park Avenue South, 5th Floor
New York, NY 10003

Ref.: Our letter to you from 9/27/99

Dear High Times !
 Here are two messages we would kindly ask you to pass on to your readers:
One concerning the Mel Frank, Trichoms, Hash Making article in High Times 4/00.
The other , VERY GOOD NEWS !

Old Hash News
Mel Frank tries again to derive " his water extraction method" from Saddhu Sam's Separating Technique.
Saddhu Sam tried to clean "GROUND GRASS" in only "COLD" water, with very little success.
Now Mel talks about "lightly crushed or rough screened .....and ice water"...and "soaking"....
In our opinion: without reference - he is using the "X-Tractor 420" recipe (Cup 97) and our
""Ice-Water-Method"",
which is much better and simpler described in High Times 5/98.

Very Good News
Save 20 to almost 50% of your power bill for your vegetative grow!
With simple clicks on you timer!
You only need 13 hours of light for excellent vegetative growth!
If you just set your timer to 12 hours of light and apply the 1 hour of light in the middle of the 12 hour
night!
Again: 12 hours ON - 5,5 hours OFF - 1 hour ON - 5.5 hours OFF..... for the vegetative cycle!
Plants love this setting and as to branch pattern prefer it to extra long work hours.
With all the power saved Hemp will already start saving the planet a little bit!
This century old trick (see Grobots manual 1992) from the flower industry is used to avoid the onset of
flowering in green houses and has only been ignored by our Bud Experts for a quarter century.

R.D. www.swissice.ch

é!

Reinhard Delp
PoBox 123
Laytonville, CA 95454, USA
Jan.21/2001

Swiss Ice Cold GmbH
Postfach 1017
CH-4502 Solothurn, Switzerland

To
Darla A. Anderson
Red Eye Press
845 W. Avenue 37
Los Angeles, CA 90065

Dear Darla

Referring to US Patent 6158591, 12/12/2000, "Method and Apparatus for Extracting Plant Resins",
I herewith respond to Mel Franks / James Goodwin's letter on his behalf from October 2. 1999.
(Copy included, I think he should have sought your advice before he sent his letter)
I find his letter extremely arrogant, but even more ignorant as to intellectual property rights.
In the letter your clients confirm:
1) That they were aware of our X- TRACTOR 4 20 and Extracting METHOD, introduced
at the Cannabis Cup 1997 in Amsterdam. (Well before their book "Hashish!" was published,
in which they introduced "Baba Bob's Aqua X - TRACTOR" !)
2) That they were aware of the fact that our method, as Patent Pending indicated, was not the
method that was published in the eighties as "Sadu Sam's Secret". Mel / James says:
"6) ...I would think that you take this as evidence that Sadu Sam's method predated yours,
since your method has improved the procedure. All Hashish-makers thank you for your input."
3) They were also aware of our business relations and agreements with Mila Jansen and the
Pollinator Co., as indicated in the High Times!- article from 5/98, which described our method
and the X-Tractor 4 20.
Despite 1-3) they continuously, intentionally and malicious infringed on our Patent rights,
promoting their book "Hashish!", as the basis of the "Ice-0-Lator", distributed by the Pollinator Co.,
while using the attention our invention had created for their own promotion and profit.
In his letter from Oct.2/99, Mel/James risks both reputations to avoid a rectification in the
Magazine "HANF!", 7/99, concerning an article, in which the reporter (Fotos: Robert C. Clarke) falsely
names Sadu Sam's recipe as the origin of the "Ice-O-lator", while promoting Robert Clarke's book.
His letter led to the suppression of our rectification at that time, in disregard of the German press law.
Your Clients actions were aiding Mila Jansen and the Pollinator Co. in her breach of our agreement,
which caused the total loss of revenue for our invention in the European Community market in the
last 3 years, since we were honoring our contract.
Also very concerning is Mel Frank's referral to commercial operations at "Trichome Technologies"
in "HIGH TIMES",4/200, using ice water temperatures in the process, infringing on our rights.
As much as we appreciate the free personal use of our method and equipment,
we have to insist on our rights as to commercial ventures!
Please inform your clients about the laws as to patents, inventions of something "New and Useful"
and the difference to copy rights, concerning reporting on other peoples ventures.
Sadu Sam's use of water might have been new at the time, like all other water experiments in
this field before him, but his restriction to traditional grinding - sifting techniques and the
ignorance about the crucial factor of ice-water-temperatur in the process made his recipe
not useful and unsuccessful for resin extraction.

Delp's 2001 response to Red Eye Press.

Your Clients were also aware of this fact.
The rapid spread of water extraction around the globe since the introduction of my
invention in 97 indicates that my invention was not only new, but is also extremely useful,
especially because of it's simplicity.
We appreciate your response, so we can work out a settlement for this matter
and ask you kindly to volunteer all information about commercial ventures of your clients,
involving water extraction of plant resins, if they are related to the US, Canada or
the European Community.
Sincerely, Reinhard Delp, Swiss Ice Cold GmbH.

PcS: www
Your clients professionalism will be finally judged by their readers, when they discover
that they were deprived of the real advantage of our method for a number of years,
- Fe. the possibility to also process fresh plant material - and are still fed obsolete
information, because of an insufficient attempt by your clients to cover up their infringement.
Mel / James thanks me in 99 for my "improvement", but still advises his readers in 2000
to keep on grinding.

Phonebook 17

SADDHU SAM'S RESIN SEPARATING TECHNIQUE

When I was in Holland last time, Saddhu Sam asked me to send High Times via this communication)

Greetings from Saddhu Sam. Cannabis aficionado extraordinaire, explorer of the mysterious universe of herbs across Africa, the Middle East, India, asia and the Americas has collected ancient secrets from growers, outlaws and mystic wanderers. This particular technique was discovered by Nevil, the King of the Cannabis Castle.

Thanks Nevil

The higher the quality of starting material, the better quality and higher the yield. There must be resin present for resin to be extracted. Water extracts more than dry sieving does.

EQUIPMENT NEEDED:

1.) Clean, coarse screen such as a window screen or strainer.

2.) Several large, wide mouth jar with screw-on lid such as one of the quart peanut butter jars.

3.) Water.

4.) Spoon and coffee filters.

HOW IT'S DONE:

1.) The material is dried over a very low heat. No higher than 90 degrees, so that it is crisp and dry.

2.) The material is ground through a coarse screen or strainer. All dust and debris is collected and not lost.

3.) Each jar is filled 1/4 way with the ground grass.

4.) The jar is filled to the top with COLD water.

5.) The lid is screwed on tight.

6.) The jar is shaken for about thirty seconds. (A blender works well for this job.)

7.) The jar is left to settle for 15 minutes.

8.) The lid is removed. Floating material is scooped out. This material is placed in a second jar and the washing process is repeated to separate any remaining resin from the material.

Sadu Sam's Resin Seperation Technique.

9.) All but one inch of the water from jar number one is gently poured off, so that the bottom layer is not disturbed.

10.) The jar is refilled with clean water and left to settle another ten minutes.

11.) All but the bottom inch of water is poured off again, leaving the bottom layer undisturbed.

12.) The water and resin remaining on the bottom is poured into an open coffee filter. Any resin remaining in the jar is washed into the filter using additional water.

13.) After all the water has drained through the filter, a spoon is used to scrape all the resin into the bottom corner of the coffee filter. At this point the resin has the consistency of wet sand. The water is gently squeezed out of the coffee filter forming the wet resin into a lump.

14.) The filter is placed inside a cloth kitchen towel to prevent it from tearing and to absorb moisture. The towel is twisted until all the moisture is squeezed out.

15.) The resin is removed from the coffee filter and flattened using the palm of one hand and thumb of the other using great pressure. The resin is placed on the heel of the palm and rolled towards the index finger. The piece is folded and the pressing is repeated over and over. The warmed resin has the consistency of well-chewed bubblegum.

16.) Mold contaminated material is cleaned using this technique. The mold neither floats nor sinks but stays in suspension in the water. To make sure all the mold is removed, growers make several extra rinsings, until the water is clear.

The water cleansing method removes virtually all debris from the glands. They are very pure. They have only the faintest taste, just an essence. The mono and di-terpenes which usually lend taste or odor have been washed away.

Smoking the material is an unusual experience. An oil pipe is used. There is virtually no smoke, just the evaporated oil. It has only the most subtle taste and no smoke, so one hardly realizes he have gotten a hit, until he feels its effects.

The resin hardens into a brittle ball when cold. However, when it is re-heated it melts and does not resolidify.

ONE GALLON
STANDARDIZED FLUID EXTRACT
CANNABIS AMERICANA

(Cannabis Sativa—American grown)

CONTAINS ALCOHOL 80 PER CENT.

PHYSIOLOGICALLY TESTED

ELI LILLY & COMPANY, INDIANAPOLIS

FL. EXT. CANNABIS INDICA.......................Dose 1 to 10 m.
Standard of Strength—That of the U. S. Pharmacopœia, 8th revision. Physiologically tested.

Cannabis sativa Linn.   Fam.—*Moraceæ.*

Synonyms—Indian cannabis U. S. P.—Foreign Indian hemp, Gunjah, Hashish, Churrus, Bhang, Subjer.

Range—Caucasus, Persia, Northern India; cultivated in Europe, Asia and the United States.

Habitat—Rich, moist soil of mountain slopes and banks of streams.

Part used—The dried flowering tops of pistillate plants.

Action and uses—NOT POISONOUS according to best authorities, though formerly so regarded. Antispasmodic, analgesic, anesthetic, narcotic, aphrodisiac. Specially recommended in spasmodic and painful affections; for preventing rather than arresting migraine; almost a specific in that form of insanity peculiar to women, caused by mental worry or moral shock. It is the best hypnotic in delirium tremens. Its anodyne power is marked in chronic metritis and dysmenorrhea. Used with excellent results in habitues of opium, chloral or cocaine. In hysterical cases not calmed by chloral or opium it acts especially well.

PREPARATION MAY 29 1913

Tincture Cannabis Indica—Fl. ext. Cannabis Indica, Lilly, 1¾ fl. ozs.; Alcohol, 14⅜ fl. ozs. Mix—Dose, 10 minims, increased till its effects are experienced.

ELI LILLY & COMPANY, LABEL REVISED 1908.

Cannabis as medicine.

Coffee shop house dealer. 600 shops catering to cannabis tourism. Marijuana is big business in the Netherlands, if estimates from the Dutch TV program *Reporter* are to be believed -- and no one is challenging them. According to the news program, the Dutch government is raking in 400 million euros (a little more than $600 million) a year in taxes from the country's 730 marijuana-selling coffee shops: estimated total sales at the coffee shops at 265,000 kilos of hashish and marijuana annually, with an annual gross revenue of about $3.2 billion in 2008.

Pollinator Co. 🌿 🌿 🌿

Amsterdam Tel ++(0)20-4708889 Nieuwe Herengracht 25

Close to scenic flee market Waterlooplein

www.pollinator.nl

SPECIALISTSHOP

16

Pleasant, post-hippie enviroment

All sizes and shapes

Meet Mila, the lady who invented the Pollinator and Ice-o-lator, tools to make excellent hash. Also smart products and seeds.

Pollinator Company. I remember Mila in India, at the time she was Jerry Shultz's girlfriend. Jerry owned Slugs Jazz Club in NYC. Mila has done real well marketing others' inventiveness. That she is considered the Queen of Hashish in Holland and Europe is a joke, and not taken seriously by the movers and shakers of the smuggling world at the time. Many of us wait to see what will happen when the Ice Wars lawsuits finally reach her doorstep.

A Hippie History

In 1973 we started Coffeeshop Mellow Yellow, the first in Amsterdam. Herman and I worked behind the bar, and Peter or Marian sat in front with a big leather bag, pretending to be "just" a customer. The bag was Peter's idea, it had sections to hold the different varieties we had for sale, all prebagged. This was the golden Coffeeshop formula, copied by many shops. A "housedealer" with different products for fixed prices. This idea made buying of H&G transparent.

37

Today the Netherlands are visited each year by millions of tourists who come to enjoy our world famous cannabis friendly society.

Peter's bag, and the Bulldog bar stool, with its secret compartment, are now on display at:

The Amsterdam Historic Museum Kalverstraat 92 or NZ Voorburgwal 359.

Mellow Yellow bag and Bulldog bar stool

Hippie History. Funny that Ben Dronker's Hemp Museum did not include a false bottom American Tourister fiberglass suitcase, thousands of which were carried by runners back in the day to Holland and around the globe. At the Mellow Yellow, hashish was available from the four corners of the planet. Amsterdam was R&R center for GIs stationed in Europe, and has been pretty much an open city where anything goes since the end of World War II.

Dutch Indoor growing instructions. As you can see the 18-6 flowering and 12-12 growing and flowering times are taught, which make no horticultural sense. In Holland in the flower industry photoperiodic control 12-1 is standard practice in controlling production costs. It would take two suns to replicate 18-6, and 12-12 makes no sense as it's neither short day nor long night. Cannabis needs a longer night to flower. Cannabis is no differently grown than poinsettia or mums. Short day-long night flowering plants. These schedules have taxed growers and consumers, and they did not even realize it till I pointed this out 30 years later. The cost to growers, over 30 years $135 billion in the US alone, who were risking there lives to grow a weed. If the Dutch flower industry went by Rosenthal or Cervantes grow books, your Mother's Day bouquet would be $3K. They paid off the status quo that owned the power companies. They lit you up like the 4th of July for law enforcement. They sold you equipment and seeds and taught you ineficient methods that caused you to spend more and grow less, while at the same time selling the mailing lists to law enforcement. From the late '80s and '90s, ordering anything from Holland became a risky venture.

Hash-making techniques. The Dutch promoting ancient techniques as their own. Both techniques can be traced back thousands of years to China.

Sinsemilla History
Past, present, future

Old Ed: 1916

Send Old Ed a postcard:

**Old Ed Holloway
p.o.Box 1491
Cave Junction
Oregon
97523 USA**

In 1979 a 63 year old American called Old Ed came to the Netherlands. He brought his seeds and tought the Dutch and therefore the Europeans how to grow Sinsemilla.

121

Today 80% of Dutch consumption of Hasj and Grass is locally grown, making home growing the best medicine against illegal import of cannabis-products from third world countries.

In the Netherlands today a lot of Sinsemilla is produced on a large scale. This product is of a poor quality and therefore mainly exported. This export will soon be reduced as more and more sinsemilla is produced in Europe. Today 50% of sinsemilla consumption in Great Brittain is already locally grown. I asume that within the next 5 years the rest of Europe will follow the Dutch role model.

Allowing some home growing for private use keeps kilo prices down and prohibits large scale production Hopefully future European politicians dare to learn from the Dutch example. You can't stop the green Cannabis avalanche, but you can avoid criminalisation by allowing small scale production.

Times have changed, and modern man, whom I like to call Homo Fantasio, hardly produces physical things anymore , but works with his mind, and therefore prefers different drugs that stimulate his brain rather than stupefies as alcohol does.

Old Ed brought seeds and taught the Dutch how to grow with the sinsemilla technique in 1979. This would blossom into the Dutch industry you see today. It really took Ronald Reagan's drug war for the homegrown market to take off. Imported hashish ruled the market in Holland until 1990 when imports were shut down to the West, and after more countries had signed international treaties.

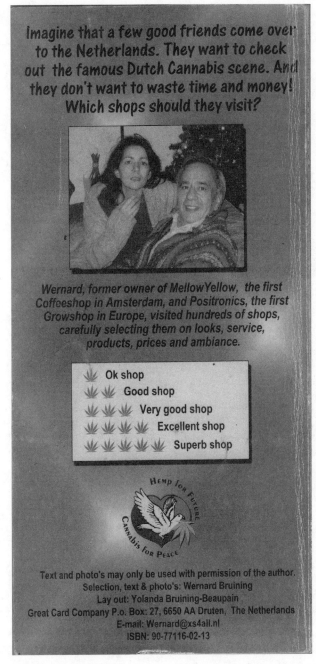

Imagine that a few good friends come over to the Netherlands. They want to check out the famous Dutch Cannabis scene. And they don't want to waste time and money! Which shops should they visit?

Wernard, former owner of MellowYellow, the first Coffeeshop in Amsterdam, and Positronics, the first Growshop in Europe, visited hundreds of shops, carefully selecting them on looks, service, products, prices and ambiance.

Ok shop
Good shop
Very good shop
Excellent shop
Superb shop

HEMP for FUTURE
CANNABIS for PEACE

Text and photo's may only be used with permission of the author.
Selection, text & photo's: Wernard Bruining
Lay out: Yolanda Bruining-Beaupain
Great Card Company P.o. Box: 27, 6650 AA Druten, The Netherlands
E-mail: Wernard@xs4all.nl
ISBN: 90-77116-02-13

Wernard Bruning the father of the coffee shop scene with his wife. The best hash was sold at the Mellow Yellow and it was the first to feature Thai sticks on its menu.

High Times Jimmy Carter cover 1978. The famous issue that outlined the betrayal of the Carter administration, by Keith Stroup of Norml.

High Times 1978 Trans High Quotations. Water hash was sold in Afghanistan for $100-170 per kilo, described as marbled. First time I saw and smoked water hash was in 1968; it was marbled with mold. I saw a few shipments that came into NYC in 1968-69; the small thin slabs that came without mold were the best anyone had seen at the time. Only when you go to Afghanistan and smoke with the Charsi do you really see how fine Afghani can get. Holland is not even mentioned; the markets in Europe in those days were in London, and Hamburg. Germany had a huge market due to all the American GI's stationed there. California seedless was $500-1000 a pound, as well as the imports it had to compete with. The big homegrown outdoor scene was in Hawaii and Alaska. Hawaiian always ruled the market, always fetched more than the best Thai, or the best anything. The Californian weed had to compete with the mountain-grown Mexican and the finest Colombian seedless, very stiff competition indeed. Then of course the different hash coming from Afghanistan, Lebanon, Pakistan, Kashmir. They had to compete with that as well. Once imports were taken off the market, only then did homegrown come into fashion: we had no other choice but to grow our own. They try and tell you the cannabis product of today is so much stronger than your grandfather's weed. It's not. When I talk a puff I can sometimes taste that old school Hawaiian in the back of who knows how many combinations they call hybrids, but it only makes me wish for the real thing. That full flavor of the Pakalolo, or that Thai flavor,. Nothing today comes close.

Head magazine – 1978

Price List

AFGHANISTAN		
Kabul Hash	oz	1-2
	lb	50-100
Marar-i-Sharif	oz	3-8
	kl	125-225
Water-pressed	oz	3-4
Hash	kl	100-200
Shirac hash	oz	5-10
	kl	150-300
AUSTRALIA		
Domestic Grass	oz	20-45
	lb	300-400
Afghani Hash	oz	100-175
	lb	1100-1700
Indian Hash	oz	70-100
	lb	800-1150
Nepalese Hash	oz	80-100
	lb	900-1300
BELGIUM		
Nigerian	oz	35-75
Black Grass	lb	450-650
Chital Hash	gm	2-3
	oz	45-70
Lebanese Hash	oz	40-60
	lb	350-600
Nepalese Hash	lb	450-650
CANADA		
Domestic Grass	oz	30-100
	lb	250-950
Regular Mexican	oz	15-25
	lb	175-275
Top-Grade	oz	35-75
	lb	450-550
Commercial	oz	35-50
Colombian	lb	300-550
Connoisseur	oz	55-85
Colombian	lb	400-700
Hawaiian	oz	200-275
	lb	2500-3000
Afghani Hash	oz	100-175
	lb	1200-1600
Indian Hash	oz	100-145
	lb	1200-1750
Kashmiri	oz	150-225
	lb	1500-2500
Afghania	gm	25-50
Hash Oil	oz	400-500
Honey Oil	gm	50-75
	oz	575-825
COLOMBIA		
Machu Picchu	oz	5-10
	lb	40-80
Santa Marta	oz	5-10
(red & gold)	lb	25-55
Colombian Hash	lb	30-60
Colombian Hash	oz	180-250
Oil	lb	2000-2500
ENGLAND		
Afghani Hash	oz	75-150
	lb	800-1400
Colombian Hash	oz	50-75
	lb	500-800
Lebanese Hash	oz	70-85
Moroccan Hash	oz	50-80
	lb	600-800
Afghani Hash	gm	25-40
Oil	oz	350-500

FRANCE		
Yamba	oz	40-60
	lb	400-600
Afghani Hash	gm	5-10
	lb	900-1100
Chitral Hash	oz	50-70
	lb	500-700
Colombian Hash	oz	35-75
	lb	450-850
Moroccan Hash	oz	25-50
	lb	350-500
GERMANY		
Afghani Hash	oz	50-75
	lb	600-800
Lebanese Hash	gm	2-5
	lb	1100-1250
Moroccan Hash	oz	35-50
	lb	450-600
Thai Sticks	one	10-20
	100	800-1200
HONG KONG		
Local Grass	oz	7-10
	lb	120-175
Thai Grass	oz	50-75
	lb	600-1000
Thai Sticks	one	10-15
Afghani Hash	gm	8-15
	oz	75-175
ISRAEL		
Lebanese Hash	oz	40-50
	lb	400-550
Local Hash	oz	20-30
	lb	250-400
ITALY		
Colombian Grass	oz	85-150
	lb	700-950
Afghani Hash	oz	100-120
	100gm	270-300
Lebanese Hash	oz	100-125
	100gm	300-350
Moroccan Hash	oz	75-125
	100gm	270-300
JAMAICA		
Jamaican Grass	oz	30-50
	lb	400-550
Coli	oz	20-25
	lb	70-100
Wild Bush Grass	oz	5-10
	lb	40-50
Local Hash	gm	50-75
Oil	100gm	500-750
MEXICO		
Guadalajara	oz	5-10
Green	lb	75-125
Guerro	oz	6-10
	lb	80-120
Oaxacan Tops	oz	3-5
	lb	50-75
Pueblo	oz	4-6
Torreon Violet	oz	5-10
	lb	80-125
THE NETHERLANDS		
Congolese Grass	oz	50-80
	lb	500-800
Domestic Hash	oz	20-40
Kashmiri Hash	oz	70-120
	lb	700-1400
Lebanese Hash	oz	50-80
	lb	500-625

Moroccan Hash	oz	50-75
	lb	400-550
Pakistani Hash	oz	50-75
	lb	500-750
Hash Oil	liter	1700-2100
TURKEY		
Antonia Hash	oz	8-10
	lb	125-200
Turkish Hash	oz	5-8
	lb	75-100
USA		
Regular Mexican	oz	20-30
	lb	120-200
Top Grade	oz	30-50
Mexican	lb	300-475
Jamaican	oz	25-40
	lb	250-400
Commercial	oz	20-40
Colombian	lb	300-425
Connoisseur	oz	40-75
Colombian	lb	350-800
Hawaiian (scarce)	oz	200-300
	lb	2200-2800
Thai Sticks	one	15-25
	oz	140-220
Empress Thai		
(scarce)	oz	200-320
Nigerian Grass	oz	40-65
	lb	600-1250
Afghani Hash	lb	1500-2000
Lebanese Hash	oz	200-250
	lb	1500-2000
Moroccan Hash	oz	100-125
	lb	1100-1500
Nepalese Hash	oz	150-225
	lb	2200-2800
Pakistani Hash	oz	150-225
	lb	2000-2300
Afghani Hash	gm	50-75
Oil	oz	450-650
Honey Oil (scarce)	gm	75-150
	oz	500-700
Lebanese Hash	gm	75-100
Oil	oz	475-625
LSD	hit	1-3
	100	75-150
Psilocybin	oz	25-35
Quaaludes	one	3-4
	100	225-300
Cocaine	gm	50-100
	oz	1200-1750
ALASKA		
Regular Mexican	oz	15-20
	lb	150-300
Domestic	oz	35-90
	lb	400-1200
Matanuska	oz	55-75
Thunderfuck	lb	500-1300
Cocaine	gr	75-130
	oz	1700-2200
USSR		
Steppes Grass	oz	40-50
	lb	400-500
Irkutsk Hash	oz	70-80
	lb	750-800
Nepalese Hash	oz	175-200
	lb	1750-2000
Tashkent Hash	oz	55-60
	lb	550-700

22 head

Head's 1978 price list. Again water hash is being sold in Kabul for $100-200 per kilo. In the 60's hashish in Kabul $5-10 per kilo. After the hash-loving King was overthrown in 1972 the prices and risks went up. Here the Netherlands is listed and as you can see very little of anything is domestic at this time.

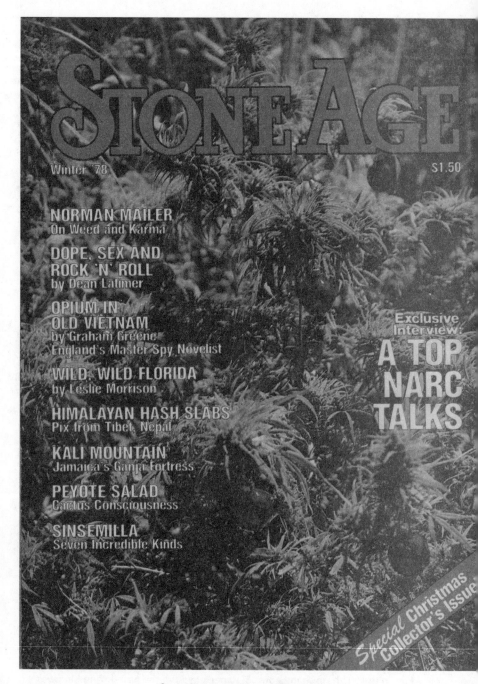

Stone Age magazine – 1978.

Mel Frank and Ed Rosenthal, first grow book – 1978.

Rosenthal ads today – The Pied Piper of Pot

Sinsemilla Schooling

Marihuana plants grown out of seeds either become female, or male. Female plants grow sticky hairs, male plants grow balls.

◀◀ If the male balls open up they spread a fine pollen. When this male pollen sticks to a female hair the plant grows a seed. If the grower removes the males, or strictly uses female klones, the desparate female plant starts to grow thousands of sticky hairs, in the hope for pollination.

◀◀ Unfertilized female flowers are called Sinsemilla. Mexican slang for without seeds. Sinsemilla Flowers are harvested, carefully dried, and smoked. ▼

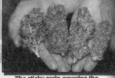

◀◀ The sticky resin covering the female plants is collected and pressed to make Hash. **68**

The Sinsemilla Story

Kees Hoekert

◀◀ In 1970 Kees Hoekert started The Lowlands Weed Company together with his friend Robbert Jasper Grootveld. The company was situated on a boat opposite an Amsterdam police station, and openly sold ten thousands of little Hemp plants. The genetics were poor, the plants grown full of seeds, but the idea was clear. The world media and millions of tourists came to Amsterdam and they spread the word: everyboddy can grow it!

In 1979 a 60 year old American, called Old Ed, came to Holland. ◀◀ He brought his seeds and tought us to grow Sinsemilla. In 1980 Wernard started the Lowlands Seed Company with Kees Hoekert as chairman. The Company produced Old Ed's seeds and a yellow photo poster explaining in Dutch the Sinsemirnilla growing technique.

In 1985 Wernard started the first growshop in Holland called Positronics, producing seeds, clones, and lights. Today 80% of sales in Dutch Coffeeshops is Sinsemilla locally grown, diminishing illegal import. **69**

Old Ed

Picture of Old Ed with Wernard and Nol Van Shok true pioneers of the Dutch scene. Ed, born in 1916, had been smoking before prohibition and was a wealth of knowledge.

High Times cover, Jorge Cervantes another Pied Piper of Cannabis, for Dutch marketing hype.

New Hashmaking Revolution, Dutch marketing hype answer to *Ice Wars*. Using stale pictures from Laurence Cherniak, this book continued the charade.

Cannabis Cup 2006

About LAURENCE CHERNIAK

Fig: 131. A canadian-born counter culture hero and artist. Laurence has over 1,000 stage, screen, radio and television productions to his credit. He served as a charter member of The Canadian Actor's Equity Assoc's Executive Board and won 1st and 2nd place in the competition to design the Can. Actor's Equity Logo. He travels extensively, speaks a dozen languages, is an ambassador at large in the cosmic world of cannabis consciousness. Dubbed "Laurence of Cannabia" by HIGH TIMES magazine. HIGH TIMES most issues ever sold, features one of Laurence's photos on that cover. LC served as HIGH TIME's only ever Intern'l Correspondent. He directed the most financially successful play in the history of the Maui Theatre "On Butterfly Wings" with 128 people in the cast; he was an actor in the last 15 minutes and had an exhibition of his paintings in the lobby. Some of his roles as a Shakespearean actor are Hamlet, Richard 2nd & 3rd, Petruchio, Othello and Marc Antony. He donated the use of his painting "My Honey & Me" to launch the 1st Annual Toronto Arts Week. It has been reproduced over 15 million times. He became a Registered Solutions Consultant with Apple Computers in 1990, photographed/published the best tribute to the 1st time ever 1992 World Series Champions, The Toronto Blue Jays. Paintings exhibited at the CN Tower in honor of the 100th anniversary of the Eiffel Tower. Laurence does very realistic portraits and can teach anyone who is interested how to paint beautiful rainbows, as seen below.

Pictures from 19th Cannabis cup.

The Responsible Cannabis Enthusiast's Guide
ABAKUS

The Mysterious Mr. Watson by Steven Hager

He was called Sam the Skunkman when I first met him, which was in Amsterdam.

Craig Copetus was the first to write about Nevil's Seed Bank operation in Holland. Nevil was a recovering heroin addict who had obtained a government grant to start a seed business as part of his recuperation. Prior to that he'd been making hash oil with a solvent and had barely survived an explosion. Nevil was a pioneer in altered states of consciousness who just happened to have a serious interest in breeding. Anyway, even though Nevil took out an ad in *High Times*, I didn't pay attention to the Seed Bank until Craig's story was published in a Washington DC magazine.

So I went off to Holland to meet Nevil, and was waylaid by Sam the Skunkman and Robert Connell Clarke immediately after that meeting happened. They wanted to give me their spin on Nevil's operation, and the quality of Dutch homegrown versus Cali homegrown, which was vast. They also let me know they'd reaped a fortune selling seeds to Nevil. Now certain disinfo agents spread the story Sam ordered me to start the Cannabis Cup so the DEA could survey growers? Truth is, Sam had no idea I'd be inventing the Cannabis Cup later that year, as I didn't even get the idea until I was on the plane home. Did Sam's stories of the Santa Cruz harvest festivals of the 1970s influence me? Of course. But Sam never presented himself as a major player in those harvest festivals, or even the boss of Sacred Seeds, or the breeder of Skunk #1, which was his primary strain. The story I got was Skunk #1 popped up unexpectedly and everybody loved it, and it won some early harvest festivals. Which is pretty much the story you get about most of the really famous strains.

When I returned to Holland for the first Cannabis Cup months later, Sam was there to greet me. He wasn't sure he wanted Cultivator's Choice, the name of his new Seed Company, to enter the first Cannabis Cup, which so far consisted of Nevil's Seed Bank and Ben Dronkers' Sensi Seeds. As I recall the Sensi Seed strains were all freshly harvested, and we couldn't smoke them without running the samples through a microwave. It would take another year for many to catch on to the importance of curing, and keep in mind some people in the industry weren't even stoners. Nevil didn't care whether he won, or whether Skunk #1 won, because he had both Skunk #1 and Northern Lights. The final decision was not Dave Watson's, but something entirely decided by grow guru Bram Frank and I because we liked the taste. The only other judge was the photographer Jiffy Schnack, who preferred Northern Lights. Nevil at the time was into dry sift made from Haze, which he kept to himself, while Sam and Robert were smoking full-melt Skunk #1, and were giddy about the way it turned to liquid when they hit it with a flame. This was all new to me.

A few years later, Arjan of the Greenhouse showed me a report by Mario Lap indicating Sam was really Dave Watson, who'd been busted in Santa Cruz one month before arriving in Amsterdam. And he'd supposedly arrived in Amsterdam with hundreds of thousands of seeds for sale one month after his bust. After selling the seeds to Nevil, who was making a fortune at the time in cash sales, Watson got the only license to study medicinal cannabis in Holland. It sure looked like Watson was secretly working with the DEA, and those operations might include tracking the IDs of all the strains of the world and documenting the growers and dealers distributing them.

I don't know if this database was real, or, if so, if it is still being pursued, but Mario claimed Watson had written a profile on the situation in Australia that named many growers and dealers.

I would not be surprised if Watson is a spook, and I can guarantee the world of illegal drugs is filled with spooks in all possible nooks and crannies. He went on to co-found HortaPharm, which made the deal with GW Pharma, which made the bigger, better deal with Bayer, the powerhouse in European medicine. Surely you realize big money is an Octopus that pulls strings everywhere it goes?

But on the other hand, I notice some trolls twisting this tale and inventing details, like Watson "ordered" me to create the Cannabis Cup so he could use the event to gather intelligence. Under that theory, you can basically end all harvest festivals or gatherings of any sort because radical conferences are always milked for intel. I started the event to create a standard for cannabis seeds, and that's exactly what happened. What Watson represented was the arrival of the West Coast hybrids into Europe.

I sure would like to interview Nevil and get his side of the story. Apparently, he became a Koi breeder for a while, and now resides in Perth.

Meanwhile all the paranoia about Watson tracking the DNA of every cannabis strain worldwide so growers everywhere would be busted is about to evaporate, isn't it? Even if they have a list in the works for the last twenty years, it won't be much good in two or three years when cannabis becomes legal everywhere.

Did you see the poll in *Time* today? Seventy-five percent of the country thinks cannabis will be legal very soon.

I'd say we're on the downside of the tipping point.

Posted online at http://abakusmagazine.wordpress.com on April 2, 2014

My first crop in Nepal, 1971. I am a General in Lord Shiva's ganja army, and it's my sworn duty to protect cannabis.

Bibliography

Campbell, Greg, *Pot, Inc.: Inside Medical Marijuana, America's Most Outlaw Industry* (New York: Sterling Publishing Co. Inc., 2012).

Clarke, Robert Connell., *Marijuana Botany* (Berkeley, CA: Ronin Publishing, 1981).

Clarke, Robert Connell, *Hashish!* (Los Angeles, CA: Red Eye Press, Inc., 1998).

Clarke, Robert C. & Merlin, Mark D., *Cannabis: Evolution and Ethnobotany* (Berkeley, CA: University of California Press, 2013).

Committee on the Judicary, Ninety-Third Congress, *Marihuana-Hashish Epidemic and its Impact on United States Security* (Washington, U.S. Government Printing Office, 1974).

ElSohly, Mahmoud, *Marijuana and the Cannabinoids* (Totowa, NJ: Humana Press, Inc. 2007).

Geluardi, John, *Cannabiz: The Explosive Rise of the Medical Marijuana Industry* (Sausalito, CA: PoliPointPress LLC, 2010).

Grotenhermen, Franjo & Russo, Ethan, *Cannabis and Cannabinoids: Pharmacology, Toxicology and Therapeutic Potential* (Binghamton, NY: The Hawthorne Press, Inc., 2002).

Herer, Jack, *The Emperor Wears No Clothes*, Eleventh Edition (AH HA Publishing, 2007).

Lee, Martin A., *Smoke Signals: A Social History of Marijuana – Medical, Recreational, and Scientific* (New York: Scribner, 2012).

Maguire, Peter & Ritter, Mike, *Thai Stick: Surfers, Scammers, and the Untold story of the Marijuana Trade* (New York: Columbia University Press, 2014).

Matthews, Patrick, *Cannabis Culture* (London: Bloomsbury Publishing Plc, 1999).

Pietri, Joseph R., *The King of Nepal: Ice Wars Edition* (Oregon: Self-published, 2006).

Pietri, Joseph R., *The King of Nepal: Life Before the Drug Wars* (Walterville, OR: TrineDay, 2010).

Preston, Brian, *Pot Planet: Adventures in Global Marijuana Culture* (New York: Grove Press, 2002).

Regan, Trish, *Joint Ventures: Inside America's Almost Legal Marijuana Industry* (Hoboken, NJ: John Wiley & Sons, Inc., 2011).

Rendon, Jim, *SuperCharged: How Outlaws, Hippies, and Scientist Reinvented Marijuana* (Portland, OR: Timber Press, 2012).

Schlosser, Eric, *Reefer Madness* (New York: First Mariner Books, 2004).

Smith, Mark Haskell, *Heart of Dankness: Underground Botanists, Outlaw Farmers, and the Race for the Cannabis Cup* (New York: Crown publishing Group, 2012).

Index

W

Z